HALLWAYS,
CORRIDORS,
& STAIRCASES

HALLWAYS, CORRIDORS, & STAIRCASES

developing the decorative & practical
potential of every corner of your home

Leslie Geddes-Brown

with photography by CHRISTOPHER DRAKE

RYLAND
PETERS
& SMALL

LONDON NEW YORK

Designer **Catherine Randy**

Senior editor **Henrietta Heald**

Location research manager **Kate Brunt**

Location research **Georgia Stratton**

Picture research **Emily Westlake**

Production **Deborah Wehner**

Art director **Gabriella Le Grazie**

Publishing director **Alison Starling**

Additional styling **Rose Hammick**

Proofreader and indexer **Alison Bravington**

First published in the USA in 2002

by Ryland Peters & Small, Inc.

519 Broadway

5th Floor

New York, NY 10012

www.rylandpeters.com

10 9 8 7 6 5 4 3 2 1

ISBN 1 84172 326 6

Library of Congress Cataloging-in-Publication Data
Geddes-Brown, Leslie
    Halls, corridors, and staircases: developing the
    decorative and practical potential of every part of your
    home / by Leslie Geddes-Brown.
        p. cm.
    Includes index
    1. Entrance halls. 2. Corridors. 3. Staircases. 4.
Interior decoration--History--20th century. I. Title.
NK2117.E5 G43 2002
728--dc21
                                        2002024944

Printed and bound in China

CONTENTS

INTRODUCTION

I came to write this book by accident. I was working on an entirely different book and had been giving a lot of thought to essential decorative treatments for the home when it struck me that the attention had been focused exclusively on the closed rooms—those cubes or rectangles closed off from the rest of the building with one or more doors. Houses and apartments have traditionally been seen as a series of reception and utility rooms—at least, in listings from realtors—but, when it comes to interior design, there is a great deal more to consider.

Between the rooms are a whole series of service areas that give access to the main spaces. They are rarely mentioned in house descriptions except in passing, because few people see them as anything but secondary to the main purpose of the building. But they are by no means secondary. For example, the foyer or entrance hall is the introduction to all that follows and, as such, is crucial in setting the scene. The stairs, too, are extremely important because they are the single element that holds the building together, floor by floor. When you arrive at the front door of a house—as a visitor or potential buyer, perhaps, or for a business meeting—you will probably come straight into the foyer, which is likely to incorporate a flight of stairs.

It is ironic that, as I write this paean to stairs, halls, landings, corridors and other unconsidered spaces, I am in a house that has no single corridor. This house is mostly medieval, and such was the lack of importance attached to privacy at the time it was built that no one had actually invented the corridor. Room led into room, and everyone walked through them. A bit earlier, staircases had also to be invented. Before that, upper rooms were reached by movable ladders, but more often, there was no upper floor, just single-height and double-height rooms, depending on how grand the building was.

So halls, landings, and corridors arrived at the time when we began to value our privacy. In 16th-century England, this meant little more than drapes around a four-poster bed while a servant slept directly behind the door—your servant was, perhaps, more familiar to you than your family—and, even in the early 18th century, servants (if you could afford them) were always nearby. Several grand English houses built around 1720 were designed with a series

RIGHT Halls are places where you welcome visitors and friends, small areas where people arrive and leave. Since they will not be lived in, they can be treated as stage sets.

FAR RIGHT Landings and corridors provide the continuity in a house. They should be designed to create a foretaste of what will happen next.

BELOW RIGHT Stairways need to be considered decoratively from many angles: from the ground up and the top floor down, from the point of view of the front door, and as people leave the house.

BELOW FAR RIGHT Entrances give the first impressions of what the rest of the house will say.

of internal corridors and rooms, entirely for the servants, who would come and go silently and invisibly in their own network of passages. It is thought that many of the fires that destroyed these early gems were encouraged by the hidden passages, which allowed the flames to spread rapidly.

True privacy arrived with the increasing wealth of the bourgeoisie in the 19th century. They could afford grand houses and plenty of servants, but they were not used to living at the center of an entire village of craftsmen, staff, visitors, and employees. The Victorian house is characterized by the sweep of the stairs, the importance of the entrance hall, and the space given to the landings on each floor.

It didn't last long. By the middle of the 20th century, when rising costs stifled urban development, space was vanishing from new houses. Stairways became narrower and steeper; halls were mere corridors, and landings were no bigger than necessary for doors to open off them. As the century advanced, it got worse, partly because people traveled more to do business and needed a place to stay wherever they worked. Big cities spread to a point where it was impossible to live on the outer edges and work in the center, and the expansion of many small towns was controlled by planning regulations.

So now, today, all our efforts and those of architects and designers are spent on maximizing the space we have. If we are clever, nothing is wasted. No landing is left bare, no corridor is just a passage from here to there, no entrance hall stays neutral. The entrance to our home sets out what is to come; it is our personal statement to visitors about what we value. Our landings have become extra rooms for whatever we need—be it book space, office space, the admiration of a special view, or a place for sewing or ironing. Corridors have taken on the role given in the 17th century to cabinets and galleries—they are where we display our collections.

The result is that every part of the house has its purpose and is made to work accordingly. No space is wasted, no square foot left unconsidered.

THE
SPACES

THE SPACES

There are more than 20 real-life case studies in this section of the book, and in the course of researching them, I found it extraordinary to discover how much variation and purpose there can be in areas primarily designed to allow access to other parts of the house.

The cases range from minute pieds-à-terre in chic areas of New York to large Modernist and country houses in the most beautiful parts of England. The dates of the case-study buildings are just as wide. These vary from a medieval hall to 18th and 19th-century town houses, 20th-century conversions of industrial buildings, and houses built this century from scratch.

During the late 20th century, as materials and techniques grew more sophisticated, stairways and entrance halls became some of the hottest architectural areas. Top architects such as Eva Jiricna and Norman Foster looked at them anew and came up with all sorts of statements in steel, wire, and glass. Many, especially those by Jiricna, are beautiful to look at, and I find

I take a deep breath, too, at such elegant solutions as the stairs in the New York apartment designed by Specht Harpman—late 20th century—and the glazed and curved corridors of the redesigned English country house built in 1937 by Raymond McGrath.

I am equally impressed by John Minshaw's reworking of an 18th-century London townhouse, which proves to me that 18th-century classical proportions can swing with the best of the modern stuff without losing any dignity—Robert Adam in Shanghai Tang, if you like—while Minshaw's friendly minimalism should inspire others to follow his lead. Although the restoration work he had to do was extensive and expensive, a less damaged house could be converted in a similar way without hideous cost.

Classic 18th-century values have been reworked in the impressive galleries and libraries curved around the walls of an early telephone exchange, where the architect was inspired by the British Museum

Reading Room. There, bookshelves were made with black-beaded cherrywood, while in a New York brownstone the interior designer stripped off layers of paint to discover such exotic wood as mahogany, rosewood, and walnut. Eger Architects changed the halls and stairs of an early 19th-century house into a 21st-century statement and a display case for modern art—demonstrating that Hawksmoor can be happy with Hockney.

Mark Wilkinson went back further into the past, attaching a timber-framed galleried extension to a 1420 building. Since the elm trees of Britain have all died and he is a man who likes tradition, he brought elm wood from America to create the floors that went with the green oak beams.

I expect that halls, corridors, and staircases will in the future get more and more glamorous treatment because the most inventive architects have taken up their cause. This is partly influenced by work in such starry interiors as chic city restaurants, fashion designers' headquarters, and rich corporate buildings. Museums such as London's Tate Modern with its huge entrance hall and Frank O. Gehry's Guggenheim Museum in Bilbao, Spain, continue to inspire more domestically inclined architects to make a statement of the entrance hall when converting old houses, while there are signs that new multistory houses really do revolve around the central core of staircase and landings leading off it.

My only caveat to these star designers is a personal one. I suffer from mild vertigo and regularly in modern buildings find I cannot go up glass staircases or down steel-ladder stairs that have no risers. A lot of people have told me that they experience the same problem—but not one of them is an architect. Since the job of designer and architect is to create buildings that are enjoyable and comfortable to use, they should pay attention to those of us who cannot climb a stair with a sheer drop and who find a banister essential to happiness. And pigs might fly.

OPULENT AND ELEGANT
BROWNSTONE CHIC

Like many people who buy houses in New York, the owners of this 1870s four-story brownstone wanted a house to themselves, but the house they loved—and later bought—had been divided into living spaces for five families.

"We wanted to live in the whole house, as a family. It therefore required major renovation," they explain. "We had to gut the entire place. We kept the front facade, but inside we chose the French Art Deco style of the 1920s, 1930s, and 1940s. We are very interested in architecture and objects of that period."

The house was a landmark building in New York, so the usual requirement would have been to restore the building in brownstone, but they were able to use limestone stucco—perhaps because there were already other examples in the neighborhood. Inside there was nothing good enough to keep, so most of it is completely new.

They called in architects DiDonno Associates. Ron DiDonno told me about brownstones: "Traditionally, the ground-floor hall was a place used almost exclusively by staff and servants, with low ceiling heights. The parlor floor, normally entered by an exterior stoop, held the most formal and elaborate spaces of the building, as well as the most formal and elaborate stairs and halls. The stairs then led up to adult sleeping spaces, and on up to the children and staff sleeping spaces, becoming less grand, and often decreasing in width and amenity, as they went. Narrow brownstones are also characterized by stairs that run along a side wall without landings or open spaces.

"In this residence, the stoop and parlor-floor entrance had previously been removed. Current governmental requirements and the clients' program did not allow us to restore them.

LEFT The main entrance, reached by several steps down from the street, leads into what was formerly a servants' area, now paved in stone parquet. The whole interior has been recreated using a series of modular, transparent walls and screens. New metal railings were specially designed and made—in period—to climb the entire height of the four-story house.

THIS PICTURE In a style reminiscent of French architecture in the first half of the 20th century, the walls lining the halls and stairways are all designed to conform to a simple grid. Some areas are made of faux limestone, while others mimic translucent windows. Colors characteristic of the Art Deco period—natural wood and cream—have been used throughout.

RIGHT AND BELOW RIGHT The stairs and banisters are an important part of the new design because, by taking inspiration from both the 1870s and the early 20th century and adding a modern twist, the entire hall and stairway area has been unified. It is often forgotten that the many floors of 19th-century townhouses need to be connected visually.

This meant that the ground-floor entry, stair, and hall were expected to provide a grander and more important introduction to the building than was normally associated with their location. Since the building lacked any remaining original detail, and the owners' program requested that the building be brought back to the detail of the 1930s and 1940s, the townhouse was renovated to house their expanding collection of furniture and objects of the period. Spatially and physically, the architecture of this period is noted for its use of transparencies, its extended spaces through glass surfaces, its use of simple forms and extensive natural light, and repetitious modular detail."

The period is also noted for its subtle use of neutrals, and this is fully exploited in the new areas. The floors are laid with flagstones of light cream that is echoed on the walls and in the stair carpet. The stairs themselves have banisters of handsome dark wood and metal rails.

One problem was a lack of light. DiDonno Associates overcame this by opening the rear dining-room wall toward the back yard. "It opened its full width to a translucent glass wall, taking in the adjacent kitchen and breakfast area. Finally, and most importantly, it introduced stair landings and turned steps, creating a modest well to extend views up and between the floors." A modular grid of faux-limestone panels was introduced, echoing the limestone of the floor and the grids of adjacent glass panels.

"A continuous, repetitious metal railing detail was used throughout, which extended up through the house." As people arrive at the living room, the panels change to glass, opening the hall to the front-facing library and rear living room. The final flourish was to create a skylight right at the top, which bathed the children's and staff bedrooms in light.

RIGHT The house lacked most of its original detail, so the architects, DiDonno Associates, took the opportunity to make large areas of the stairway walls into windows, adding to the light and space between the stairs and the rooms.

BELOW Interior windows—with glazing bars similar to those on the exterior—have been installed between landings and the rooms beyond, unifying the entire house.

OPPOSITE The architects not only took inspiration from the 1920s and 1930s, but also used materials typical of the period. Translucent and transparent glass, popular in the early 20th century, has been imaginatively used both to provide light in the stairwell and to bring the rooms into the scheme.

USE OF SIMPLE FORMS, EXTENSIVE NATURAL LIGHT, AND REPETITIOUS MODULAR DETAIL IS CHARACTERISTIC OF EARLY 20TH-CENTURY ARCHITECTURE.

LEFT Great designs from the mid-20th century have been used to furnish this City of London flat, reflecting the period of its building. Characteristic 1960s Japanese grass paper covers an interior wall.

RIGHT The entire apartment is a long rectangle with exterior windows at both ends—the owner lives in a corridor. Yet space and style have been created by clever use of lighting at all levels—here it has been installed underneath the bookshelves as well as hidden in the ceiling.

FAR RIGHT Since the apartment is located at the top of the multistory building, the architects have been able to steal daylight from the stairwell through a translucent door. This area has a lowered ceiling to accommodate the sleeping platform.

SIXTIES SANCTUARY
DESIGNED FOR PRACTICAL LIVING

The Barbican complex—which grew from a bombed site in London's financial district—incorporates apartments, shops, restaurants, an arts center, and public gardens. It has a reputation for impenetrability, but this does not include the light and airy apartments, stacked up in towers. The flat featured here is a long rectangle with windows at both ends—a hall or galley-type space into which everything must be shoe-horned—but it has the advantage of being a penthouse with a strong, barreled-roof feature.

The Belgian owners called in Jo Hagan of USE Architects, who remodeled this difficult space with a practical, sculptural elegance in keeping with the architecture. The front door opens almost immediately onto the main room, which is flooded with light. From its enormous window, the owners have an exciting view of the constant work of tearing down and building up of new offices that characterizes the City of London—and of the wonderful dome of St. Paul's Cathedral beyond.

A small bedroom has been put on a platform to save space in the corridor below, and this is reached from a precarious but abstract ladder stair, cantilevered out of the wall. A small office fits underneath, with a lower ceiling and the other main window. Everywhere there is 1960s' furniture and such decoration as grass cloth wallpaper—all in keeping with the original architecture. Since the entire apartment is so open and so limited, flush-fitting double doors hide the kitchen, which is lit from a skylight. Similarly, the entrance area borrows light from the brightly lit top of the stairwell by means of two internal windows. Clever use of storage, space, and particularly light turns this difficult apartment into a triumph of style, while keeping it authentically in period.

OPPOSITE Although this welcoming hall and its stairs are part of a London house, the atmosphere is determinedly rural (and not only because of the dog). The architecture is spacious, with the sense of a large backyard beyond, emphasized by the presence of outdoor impedimenta such as hats, umbrellas, and boots. The simplicity of the coloring and plain runners is also rural in spirit. The neat desk tucked by the stairs is used by the owners as an extra office and storage space.

LEFT A hall is the perfect place for hanging outdoor clothes, bags, and bulletin boards. The trick is to make them look good. In this case, someone in the house clearly has a passion for raffia, grass, and straw, which happily suit the off-white color scheme.

BELOW Working equipment and supplies—boots, brooms, brushes, and logs stacked ready for winter fires—are combined in a charming corner by an outside door.

FAMILY HOME
IN RUSTIC STYLE

There's an awful lot of pretension and pomposity in the interior design world, where the big cheeses can cheerfully charge $50,000-plus for designing a single room—which might then prove uninhabitable. It is delightful, therefore, to come across someone like Vivien Lawrence, an erstwhile professional cook and party-giver who has now moved into the design field. Did she have training for any of this? Not at all. Her training was cooking, entertaining, decorating, and living for herself.

The large family house in London that Vivien redesigned and decorated exemplifies her approach to life. It is comfortable, relaxed, and practical, and it can be altered to suit the owners' changing circumstances.

The house was built at the end of the Edwardian era, that most English of periods, when homes began to change from high Victorian palaces run by teams of servants into the modern refuges familiar to us today. It was designed by an architect who worked with Sir Edwin Lutyens, who was himself greatly influenced by vernacular English building styles. So, while the rooms are spacious and grand, with materials of the best quality and detailing of the highest possible standard, the whole house is friendly and accessible.

Like many such houses, it had fallen on hard times; and its essential style, which had become unfashionable, was hidden under layers of disguise. "When I first saw the house, it was nothing like this," Vivien Lawrence says now. "So I did a lot of research into what it would have been like in that period." This is reflected in such old-fashioned features as large meat plates poised on high shelves in the hall—the *denier cri* around 1910.

The real charm of this house is that, while it is located in one of Britain's most urban areas, it seems as though it could be in the country. All the rooms overlook the yard, and you can't see the road from anywhere—just the yard itself and the green spaces beyond. The decor is very much English country style. "Even though I do everything, I am perhaps most confident with this style," says Vivien Lawrence. "I do very modern stuff—which so many people are after now—but I do like old dark furniture with traditional white decoration and contemporary touches."

What is notable about the house is how everything blends together. This was a conscious decision. "When the owners moved in with five children, they were looking for somewhere with a lot of light, an openness. The whole house is very light and countrified. The stairs and landings had plenty of niches to sit in, and TVs were put in some of these parts for the use of the children and their friends."

Now, all but the youngest child have left home, and their sitting and meeting places have been reworked by the designer into areas where party guests can mingle and huddle. "The owners do a lot of entertaining, and they set up a buffet in the dining room. Guests can get their meals, walk through, and sit and eat all around the house." To make them comfortable, there are sofas and squashy chairs everywhere. There's a sofa and armchair in the big kitchen, another sofa on the upstairs landing, two in the living room, plus an armchair and more chairs in the hall and dining room.

LEFT The date of this elegant London house—1910—and the influence of Sir Edwin Lutyens in its design are evident in the space, detailing, and vernacular touches of the relaxed but imposing foyer. Light floods in through a glass door leading outside and from a large staircase window. Already welcoming, the area has been made even more friendly by its light coloring and the addition of a log basket and an overstuffed chair.

ABOVE At the back of the house is a lavish garden whose scents and colors often make their presence felt indoors.

BELOW AND RIGHT Part of the house's charm lies in the muted tones of its decorative schemes and the way in which odd corners have been turned into places where visitors can lounge and chat. The dinner plates arranged on a high shelf are an authentic detail from the Edwardian period.

Vivien Lawrence was keen to make every space work. As a result, the foyer has been designed to double as a small office-cum-party-space. "It's made so that people can sit there. There's a fireplace, with a pitch pine surround that I found somewhere—I do a lot of looking around for my clients—which has a coal and gas working fire. There are also two armchairs, bookcases, and a desk. It's also got a nice wood floor."

The wide stairs have panelling below the dado and, typically, are dog-legged from a low level, allowing the desk to fit neatly in the corner. Windows let in the maximum light, for they have

shutters rather than curtains. More light comes in from glazed doors and from the fact that both walls and balusters are painted clear white. The characteristic parquet floors of the hall and the stairs are covered in light neutral matting.

Each part of the Edwardian building is used to the full—for the owners, their large family, and all their friends. The lesson is that stairs, landings, corridors, and halls are perfect for entertaining lots of people, and just as good for a big family with many different interests—all its members can have a space to themselves and their enthusiasms without feeling shut away from everyone else.

OPPOSITE, MAIN PICTURE AND INSET Landings and halls have been designed for lounging and talking. Here an upstairs landing has been given a squashy sofa—heavily cushioned for extra luxury—and a helpful reading light. The scene just asks for conversation pieces.

ABOVE AND ABOVE LEFT A random selection of everyday objects such as traditional watering cans, gardening tools, barbecue equipment, and old-fashioned terra-cotta pots—to say nothing of a comfortable pair of old clogs—has been used to spice up the character of an odd space and point the way to the garden. Giving working spaces a distinctive style is a current preoccupation among designers—and these brick-lined passages show how it should be done.

ALTHOUGH THIS HOUSE IS LOCATED IN ONE OF BRITAIN'S MOST URBAN AREAS, IT HAS A DISTINCTLY RURAL FEEL THAT OWES MUCH TO ITS STYLE OF DECOR.

BOOKS, PAINTINGS AND SCULPTURES IN A
FLEXIBLE HALLWAY

ABOVE Lateral thinking is needed to break out of the style straitjacket imposed on London townhouses built in the Georgian era. Here, at the back of the house, the typical entrance arch has been modernized to create a garden door, adding space and light to the ground-floor hallway, which has been redesigned to make a library. The heaviness of the bookshelves is offset by the soothing blues, grays, and whites used to decorate this part of the house and the soft French limestone pavers that cover the floor.

Dick Cooper's brief to Eger Architects was to get far more light into his early 19th-century house. "Curiously," he says, "it was quite late in the restoration when we decided to do this. I'd seen a house under the London Open House scheme—in which owners open their houses to the public—that had lots of light coming in from above, and this encouraged me."

The hall in this handsome late Georgian house was a front-to-back corridor set a few steps above street level in a single story attached to the main building—so the decision to put a skylight above the front door was "obvious."

The corridor widens as it runs from front to back, and when the Coopers arrived, the wide end was occupied by a defunct bathroom. The architects removed it and reinstated a back door, with a metal bridge leading over the basement area to the garden beyond.

A new bathroom was installed above the corridor at second-floor level. Another bathroom was built above that—an amazing confection of glass, rather like a conservatory, says Dick. Then the wider end of the corridor, beside the back door, was lined with hefty bookshelves painted a dark slate color.

Everywhere else is painted in Dulux's Cornflower White, which is, in fact, a very soft gray/blue. The floor is a pale neutral beige. But the architect John Eger had more tricks to play with the light. A big secondhand mirror, 24 in (60 cm) high and 8 in (20 cm) wide, which once adorned the side of a 16-wheeler, has been mounted on the fifth-floor parapet. "It's angled so that, if there's any sun in the evening, it'll bounce into the hall. It's apparently an idea Alvar Aalto came up with," says Dick Cooper. "I'm also a great enthusiast for John Soane—the Soane Museum in London is full of mirrors. So I put mirrors all

THIS PAGE Dick Cooper is an enthusiastic collector of modern paintings and sculpture. A small work by Richard Devereux is visible through the arch, and another of Devereux's paintings hangs above the door in the photograph on the opposite page. Genuine Georgian arches are featured throughout the stairway area of the house—but the one behind the dark blue bookshelf has simply been painted onto the wall.

THIS PAGE The configuration of this London house—the front door is positioned on one side of the main building—meant that the architects could introduce extra light into the normally dark area behind the front door by adding a skylight. The firm, Eger Architects, also added shallow niches echoing the shape of the Georgian arched front door. What appear to be broken arches on each side of the corridor are in fact Italian uplighters. The sculpture of a hand was made by Mark Dunhill, a brother of one of the owners.

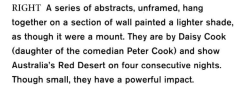

RIGHT A series of abstracts, unframed, hang together on a section of wall painted a lighter shade, as though it were a mount. They are by Daisy Cook (daughter of the comedian Peter Cook) and show Australia's Red Desert on four consecutive nights. Though small, they have a powerful impact.

BELOW RIGHT The house is full of modern works of art, which combine surprisingly well with the early 19th-century interior. The portrait head in terracotta is of the owners' 14-year-old son, who commissioned Rosemary Shepherd to make it as a present for his parents. The abstract is by Mark Shepherd.

around the edges of the skylight. They are 4 in (10 cm) deep and bounce the light around the hall. People who don't know the house say the appearance of the skylight is deceptive, and they can't define where the glass is. There's also a spotlight outside, on an extension roof, which shines through the skylight at night like the moon."

Built when Egyptian style was in fashion, the south London house has splayed marble fireplaces. Dick Cooper has taken up this theme in, for example, a splayed cut-off obelisk supporting a clay bust of his son. The elegant architecture is emphasized by the deep blue walls inside the original arched embrasures. Their line is followed through in faux arches—simple paint jobs—and the painted arch over the back door.

The hallway area is perfect for showing off Dick Cooper's collection of modern art—"I spend money on art, not clothes"—which varies from the traditional bust of his son to abstracts by Daisy Cook, daughter of the comedian Peter Cook, and castings by his brother-in-law, Mark Dunhill, a professor of sculpture.

The whole hallway is both practical and extremely stylish, from the solid dark bookshelves that frame the yard beyond the back door to the sharply hung paintings and sculptures. The combination of the palest blue with deeper blue arches, real or faux, emphasizes the cool architecture. The open arch, which leads into the main body of the house, seems therefore to be perfectly logical, especially as the blue coloring is extended to the underside of the plain, white staircase glimpsed beyond.

THE WHOLE HALLWAY IS BOTH PRACTICAL AND EXTREMELY STYLISH, FROM THE SOLID DARK BOOKSHELVES THAT FRAME THE YARD BEYOND THE BACK DOOR TO THE SHARPLY HUNG PAINTINGS AND SCULPTURES.

ABOVE LEFT **Foyers usually end up as working spaces—centers of activity where packages arrive and coats are hung. The trick is to keep the clutter generated by such activity under control. The owner of this rural English home uses handsome French baskets casually popped into corners to hold less elegant items.**

ABOVE **Grouping pictures takes skill. Here, they are ranged around a wall light, and though quite different in style and subject, they are unified by the use of cool colors and sketchy artistic treatment. The colors of the sketches, mats, chairs beneath, and paintwork are so cleverly considered that they seem entirely natural.**

BLUE-GRAY PALETTE IN A
NATURAL HAVEN

The generous entrance hall of this farmhouse-style home in rural Gloucestershire is lined with numerous doors that promise exciting glimpses of other rooms. An unseen window overhead has the effect of flooding the whole area with natural light. And then there are the stairs. They are perfect. From a wide bottom step they arch in a gradual curve, rather than a brutal dog-leg angle, gently toward the light. An equally elegant iron banister with the minimum of ornament follows the curve, while the area under the stairs is the plainest of walls.

Many people would have been tempted to overdecorate this wonderful space. But not the present owner, who has introduced a controlled and disciplined color palette that hints that the sea may not be far away.

Taking inspiration from the soft gray of the treads and risers of the stairs, she has colored all the doors, their frames and the baseboards in the same misty gray-blue. Elsewhere, where the doors are surrounded by large blocks

of local stone, this has been left untouched. The floor is entirely unadorned—not a single rug—but colored in the same shade, leaving the lines of the floorboards to lead the eye toward the curving stairs and to emphasize the generosity of the area.

The walls are hung with groups of pictures that are simply framed, though no attempt has been made to match them. Many have mats the same colors as the woodwork and all are sketchy rather than overworked. Below them are ranks of chairs, some matching but colored differently, others adorned with similar cushions and upholstery. The whole appears casual, with shoes and baskets posed where they seem to have dropped. But such relaxation is achieved only through enormous care—and scrupulous neatness.

Discipline, a refined color sense, and the ability to make best use of the architecture all come together in this hall. What's more, the combined effect is to give visitors a fine welcome.

THIS PAGE The owner of this rustic haven enjoys the combination of ranged chairs with paintings above. Again, the pictures are similar in weight and color, and hung around a wall light, but as befits the main hall, the chairs themselves are more intricately designed. A major influence on this friendly hall is the light that floods in from above. Its source cannot be seen, but the effect is to emphasize the stairs and make them inviting. More, almost hidden, pictures also ask the visitor to come upstairs.

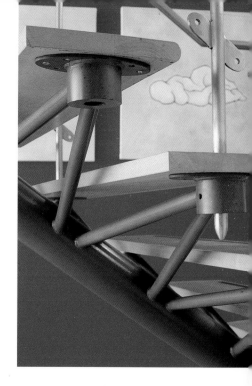

LEFT AND OPPOSITE The curvaceous stairs were a major element in the apartment's design, as carried out by Zynk Design Consultants. The purpose was to create a stylish and open series of steps which, because the treads are of warm maple wood, is friendly rather than daunting. The curves add to the sensuous feeling in the apartment—while, more practically, allowing large pieces of furniture to be easily moved up and down.

RIGHT A detail of the maple treads on their mild steel supports shows the precision and care with which the stairs were designed. Their profile is accentuated by the strong red wall and modern painting just behind.

AIRY AND CURVACEOUS
LOFT SPACE

David Vanderhook is a busy chef who needs plenty of room to incorporate not only a generous kitchen, but also an office, as well as lots of room for entertaining—so he set out to find as large an apartment as possible. At 2,500 sq ft (230 sq m), Vanderhook's London loft has more space than the average five-bedroomed house.

He bought it as a shell from a developer who had decided that spiral stairs would be the answer to moving between floors. Indeed, spiral stairs had been put in other lofts in the building. But Zynk Design Consultants, who worked with Vanderhook on the project, preferred a different solution.

"They said that, with ceilings 13 ft (4 m) high, the spiral would need to turn back on itself—and when that happens you start to get dizzy going up and down. They proved it by taking me into another apartment in the building."

Spiral stairs are also problematical when moving furniture—and, in a space as large as David Vanderhook's, you need substantial pieces—so the hole that had been cut into the floor to accommodate the spiral staircase has been transformed into a glass bull's-eye and new stairs have been built.

The present staircase is curvaceous and modern without being daunting. The treads are made of warm maple wood, while the airy banisters, handrail, and supports for the treads were specially made of mild steel.

Cut-off white walls—more like screens, really—were carefully sited so that working areas could be concealed behind them. "Having an office behind one wall at the top of the stairs means that the area can be as messy as I choose to leave it. The curved screen in front gives the impression that it's part of the apartment while at the same time, somehow, out of it. The whole idea here is

to keep the sense of spaciousness and to have an abundance of curves, which can work very well in large areas."

Vanderhook and Zynk also had fun with the lighting and colors in the space. While much of the loft is plain white, there are strong splashes of color, including bold terra-cotta red behind the minimalist stairs. On this is hung a set of oil paintings—clouds on a vivid blue sky—by Trevor Thomas, an artist acquaintance of Vanderhook. Another trio of paintings by Thomas hangs in formation on the white wall that screens the office. This has evocative memories for Vanderhook. "It's called 'Sunset in Wadi-Rum.' Wadi-Rum is in Jordan, where I used to work for King Hussein." The trio is also strongly colored and picks up the terracotta shade of the wall below.

The lighting is both modern and ingenious. Simple egg-shaped shades, which hang above the staircase, are made of porcelain and give soft, diffused lighting. Above them is a set of lights, from a system called Cyclops. Elsewhere, fiber-optic lights have been sunk into the floors and buried to create backlighting in the risers of the first few stairs.

Along with the sets of colorful paintings and contrasting walls, the area has also been given a series of asymmetric niches—squares and rectangles to contrast with the curving walls. Some of these are used for display—a spiky cactus glowers from one—while others are empty. In response to the artificial lighting or the natural daylight that floods in through the area's generous windows, these are capable of transforming themselves into minimal abstracts in the manner of Victor Pasmore.

The whole apartment—a skillful collaboration between owner and designers—is not only stylish but practical. "It's just perfect," says David Vanderhook.

"THE WHOLE IDEA IN THIS GENEROUSLY PROPORTIONED LOFT IS TO MAINTAIN THE FEELING OF SPACIOUSNESS AND TO HAVE LOTS OF CURVES, WHICH CAN WORK WELL IN LARGE AREAS."

OPPOSITE David Vanderhook's office is concealed behind a half-screen that matches the plain white walls of the stairway. The eye is led away from the screen by the asymmetrical niches on the wall beyond. Three paintings of Jordan, grouped up the staircase, have the same effect. Showing a sunset in Jordan, they remind David of the time when he worked for King Hussein.

THIS PAGE A group of paintings by Trevor Thomas show clouds against a clear blue sky and just demand to be hung against a strong red wall. The base of the staircase consists of three generous wooden steps into which fiber-optic lights have been set. The steel banisters are perfectly proportioned in this friendly, but minimalist, loft space.

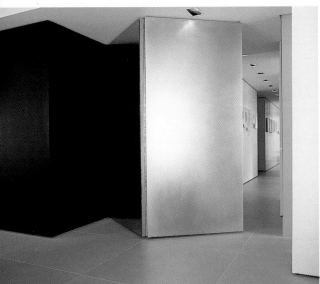

CITY RETREAT
WITH ORIENTAL TOUCHES

Michael Gabellini had two particular advantages when it came to designing this New York apartment: he is an architect with a strong sense of how to organize space, and his client is an avid collector of photographs, from the earliest Fox Talbots to modern prints. The photos are displayed with maximum simplicity and drama—and they dictate the style of the rest of the apartment.

The space is generous, with three open aspects—to north, south, and west—and two roof terraces. Light had to be targeted to enhance enjoyment of the photographs without damaging them. This was achieved by a series of movable partitions linked by a spine passage. With his use of subtly grained dark wood, stainless steel, glass, and a palette of neutral off-whites, it is clear that Michael Gabellini has been influenced by Japanese buildings, which often contain movable partitions. The few ornamental details—woven pillows and sandals of rush—are also Japanese. Much else in the apartment, where corridors become rooms and rooms turn into halls, can be adapted to suit the moment. Glass partitions between bathrooms and bedrooms can be changed from opaque to transparent by the flick of a switch; a large photograph hangs on a wall that turns into a sliding screen hiding the television.

Gabellini not only designed the space, but also created much of the furniture. The materials used depend on multicultural influences, and help to create an apartment that is at once austere and warm.

ABOVE LEFT The confined elements of this streamlined apartment have been made satisfyingly adaptable by the installation of movable partitions. These mean that the apartment can be changed from a calm and private haven into a series of flowing spaces.

LEFT The owner collects photographs by 19th- and 20th-century masters. These are hung in matching frames at eye level but without any serious attempt at grouping. Natural light adds interesting shapes and shadows.

ABOVE Minimalist design has been used to create drama and space. Light-painted walls are lit, while dark ones are left in shadow. Despite the almost complete lack of objects, the corridor beckons enticingly.

OPPOSITE The whole area is linked together by a central spine, along which load-bearing columns and moving screens are all worked to the same module. A constant theme is the honey-colored stone that has been used on all the floors.

LEFT Georgian townhouses are surprisingly adaptable to utterly plain modern schemes. Here, subtle shades of white have been used throughout. The table was designed in the tradition of the master of Art Deco, Jacques Emile Ruhlmann; its top is made of Belgian fossil marble with charcoal lacquer and silver leaf beneath.

BELOW LEFT The designer John Minshaw, who owns the house, was able to prove that its windows were not original. After a fight with the "heritage" authorities, he was allowed to replace them with lighter and airier modern versions. Since the house lacked any backyard, Minshaw also created a small orangery at the back.

CLASSIC GEM
REVIVED IN ITS ORIGINAL STYLE

John Minshaw, of John Minshaw Designs, is, he tells me firmly, "an interior architect." "We are not decorators; we are designers and, after seven years at art school and running my own factory, it peeves me greatly to watch those house makeovers on television and hear people saying they're decorators."

Minshaw's general style is to strip the houses he buys and to reinvent the pure architecture, if it's there—or, if it's not, to create authentically researched period details. He uses many neutral shades as a background for "stonking great antiques." This is exactly what he's done at his own early 19th-century house in central London.

When he bought the house, the plan was to develop it and sell it on: "It definitely wasn't a love purchase." When he first saw the five-story building, it had been lived in by tenants who had "trashed" it. They had put up flocked wallpaper everywhere and added a disco and bars "in every corner."

"We had been beaten out twice on other beautiful houses —one by Robert Adam. I'd already seen this house and decided there was no way I would take it on—it was in such a state. But then the price tumbled and my intention was to bring it up to scratch and sell it. But, as we opened up the house, it became filled with light. We'd bought it in winter, and the light came with the spring. In fact, it's the most extraordinarily light house in which I've ever lived. When I saw this, I told the builders to restart their work and improve the quality of everything—and the house came into itself. I just love it now."

It was built around 1810, but to a pattern-book design that is clearly much earlier. "It's on the Portman estate, one of five in a row. The Victorians had flounced it up a bit, with egg and dart plasterwork, but we put in Tuscan moldings." Apart from the

THIS PAGE Although the house dates from 1810, it was clearly modeled on earlier Georgian pattern books. Typically for central London, the entrance hall and stairs are very spacious—far more than in other town houses of the same period built further from the city center. It was John Minshaw's idea to add glass to the paneled screen that hides the basement stairs.

stairs themselves, virtually everything is new—though it doesn't look it. "There was a Victorian window at the top and, below that, a 1930s window. The authorities wouldn't allow us to take them out, saying they were original. But, on appeal, we were able to prove that the earlier window's joints were Victorian, not Georgian." The stairs are now lit by a new window over 14 ft (4 m) high, which is, says Minshaw, "pure Georgian" in style and completed with the thin glazing bars typical of the period.

The stairs—which go down a story from the main door to what was once the servants' basement and rise another four flights to the top of the house, where the servants would have slept—are made, unusually, of stone. They are virtually without decoration, as are the banisters and polished-mahogany handrail. "They had had years of abuse but were made to an extremely simple design. The balusters are made of metal, which means they are thinner than if they were of wood. They were sandblasted to a dull, polished metal and the stone cleaned as much as possible."

The stairs are generously wide with plain but elegant curves, starting with a flourish on the ground floor. They can be seen immediately you enter the house's wide, plain hallway, which has been given a new wooden floor. A console table, designed by Minshaw, stands against a wall. "I designed and made that table. It's of charcoal lacquer with a Belgian fossil top and silver leaf at the bottom. It was extremely expensive to make, and we only did three of them. It's an ode to Ruhlmann."

OPPOSITE Unlike many London houses, this fine example has real stone stairs. Although the stairs had been appallingly treated over the centuries, Minshaw was able to clean them to an acceptable level. The stairs extend from below ground, a flight down from the main entrance, up another four flights. Walls flanking the stairs are all painted in shades of white—except on the top floor, which bursts into purple.

THIS PAGE A window on the staircase turned out to be much later than the date of the house, so Minshaw was allowed to replace it with a modern "Georgian" one that is more than 14 ft (4 m) high. It has the fine glazing bars typical of the 18th century and lets in huge amounts of light. The metalwork suspended from the ceiling is a 19th-century Indian oil light complete with gimbels, which once hung outside a shop.

LEFT AND BELOW LEFT AND RIGHT
The best schemes rely on fine tuning of details—and this is what makes Minshaw's house exceptional. The metal banisters, which are original to the house, are far finer than they would be in wood and have been sandblasted to a flat metallic finish. The simple mirror hangs above the living-room door to reflect light and echo the line of the stairs. Though the whole scheme is based on white, at least three shades have been used, all from Sanderson. These include Dusky White, Oyster White, and a greenish-white limewash. Even necessary fixtures have been carefully sited and made of steel to fit the blanched whole.

"AS WE OPENED UP THE HOUSE, IT BECAME FULL OF LIGHT. WE'D BOUGHT IT IN WINTER, AND THE LIGHT CAME WITH SPRING."

One thing the house lacked was a backyard—a disappointment for Minshaw after his previous house in Primrose Hill. "We felt a bit claustrophobic with the little 'mews' street directly at the back." The answer was to make a little orangery on the ground floor at the very end of the house, which can be seen from the main front door and gives interest and light at the end of the stairway corridor. "It's all new. When we bought the house, it was part gym and part kitchen. It's been very successful, sunny all day long." Carefully positioned in the light, and visible from the stairs, is an exuberantly decorated iron chair, an Italian antique of about 1840, upholstered in off-white.

The whole area is painted in three or four different off-white shades, many in flat oil, which he uses a lot. "It's an old designer's trick. If, for example, you paint a horizontal ceiling a lighter shade, it will appear the same as the walls." Here the shades include Sanderson's Dusky White and Oyster White, both with a touch of green in the white, which, he says, gives the effect of authentic limewash.

Just when you are beginning to think that John Minshaw is too good to be true, he admits to a little joke. At the very top of the house, where the stairs suddenly deteriorate in quality—they were once used exclusively by servants—the soft whites on the walls turn to a dark purple, definitely not an authentic Georgian color. "It's a dark little space, leading up to two bedrooms," Minshaw comments. "There was no way we could make it light so, as a joke, we made it a really dark color."

THIS PAGE When John Minshaw first saw the house, it was in a terrible state after a long period of neglect. Although what can now be seen appears to be pure Georgian, much of the detailing was replaced by him. The view from the living room shows immaculate reeded door frames with paterae and a calm parquet floor. The stairs still show the marks of old paintwork, but they are now venerably distressed.

PIED-À-TERRE
THAT MAKES MAXIMUM USE OF SPACE

Suze Orman is a financial consultant and writer who divides her time between California—her main home—and New York, where she has a tiny pied-à-terre. For her architects, Mullman Seidman of New York, the trick was to create, in a space no bigger than 818 sq ft (76 sq m), a home with the same feeling and atmosphere as the one in California. Suze Orman also needed her New York home to reflect her interests there—entertaining, meditating, and staying in constant touch with the global financial world.

"Our design goal was to make this small apartment seem spacious rather than cramped," Patti Seidman explains, "and to accommodate at least a scaled-down version of the lively variety of activities Suze enjoys in her California house. To make them feel bigger, the spaces were kept very open to one another, and the color scheme throughout the apartment is harmonious and low contrast." These colors are a series of soft blues interspersed with a variety of whites, creams, and taupes. The wooden floors are a darkish shade of mahogany, with variations of texture, including plain, vertical boards and herringbone parquet. In between—apparently breaking up the sweep of the wood but, curiously, keeping the flow between the rooms intact—is a floor of small blue terrazzo tiles. These delineate the bathroom, whose walls are covered with more of the same tiles. It's as though an area of sky blue, textured and slightly

ABOVE LEFT Really tiny apartments often draw gasps of admiration at the ingenuity with which all essentials have been shoehorned into the space. One way in which the designers were able to achieve this was to make the spaces work twice. The guest bedroom is normally the apartment's foyer with the bed hidden in a cupboard.

ABOVE Although this New York apartment is a second home, the owner wants to be able to work and entertain here fully. Space has even been allowed for artworks.

RIGHT Apparent space is created by making each room lead into another, giving light, interest and distance. Here, the bedroom doors are flung open to show the dining area beyond. Since the apartment is like a circle, you can walk around it in either direction, getting different views and angles depending on which way you go.

THIS PAGE When planning to live in a tiny space, you need to get rid of preconceptions and prejudices. The designers of this eyrie decided that the bathroom was central to the whole plan. This vista takes in the sculptural chairs of the dining area and adds a glimpse of the bathroom before homing in on the comforts of the living room beyond. Note how every space is utilized—there are even drawers under the sofa.

OPPOSITE, LEFT The whole apartment has been unified by using a strictly controlled range of colors—plenty of natural wood for floors, doors, and built-in furniture. Elsewhere walls are soft white—except for the central bathroom, which is cool blue and located so it can be reached from the main bedroom, the guest room, or the living areas.

OPPOSITE, RIGHT When colors are strictly controlled, it's a good idea to incorporate different textures. Thus the bathroom, pivotal to the whole plan, is covered in mosaic tiles of a calm sky blue. These are even used in the floor, which breaks up the vista from room to room and adds variety.

COLOR, STORAGE, AND FURNITURE ARE PLANNED AND SITED TO CREATE FOCAL POINTS THAT LEAD THE EYE INTO SUCCEEDING ROOMS AND BEYOND.

glittering, is interposed between the main receiving rooms. The single bathroom was put beside the receiving rooms for a good reason: the foyer has been designed to double as a guest bedroom.

"The circulation space had to be efficient and multifunctional," says Patti Seidman, "so the foyer becomes a spare bedroom, by means of a Murphy bed that looks like a hall closet when not in use. To provide guests with a modicum of privacy, the closet doors fold back to screen the hall from the living area." This is a very neat idea, for the opened cupboard doors create a wing at each side of the bed.

The bathroom can be used by guest and owner alike without either getting in the other's way. "Guests have access to the bathroom without having to walk through the main bedroom. The bathroom also connects the bedroom to the kitchen/dining area, offering an alternative path that makes the apartment feel bigger than it actually is." In fact, it has been made into a continuous walk that means people don't have to double-back on themselves.

A sensation of space also comes from the vistas that have been created from one room to the next—people can look from the living room through the dining area and all the way to the far side of the bedroom. "A lot of attention was paid to the color and composition of what can be seen of the adjacent space through the doorway." The result is that color, storage, and furniture are planned and sited to create focal points that lead the eye into succeeding rooms and beyond. Intriguing touches tempt one to walk through to see more.

The kitchen is compact but very well equipped. A very large coffee table and floor pillows were chosen with informal dinner parties in mind. The effect of overscaling some of the furniture is to make the space seems correspondingly larger. "The circulation in the kitchen is also the way to the dining area and an alternate way to the living room," says Patti Seidman. "Built-in custom cabinetry in the kitchen continues into the living area, where it holds television and stereo equipment, as well as the computer, printers, and fax required to run a sophisticated home office."

OPPOSITE Halls and landings can be cool and minimalist, but at different periods they may take on great power and grandeur. This two-story wood-framed hall was built by master craftsman Mark Wilkinson using the methods of medieval builders. A vast extension was added to a much more modest, genuinely early house, whose outside wall, wood-framed in squares, can be seen on the right of the photograph.

RIGHT When dealing with the huge spaces which medieval builders allotted to banqueting halls and domestic manorial courts, everything has to be scaled to match. Thus the open galleries that run around the main hall are ranged above a dramatic fireplace. Instead of the normal wooden lintel, Wilkinson has used a gigantic boulder quarried from the land above his house. It was then cut down to only 18 in (45 cm) deep and set in concrete.

BELOW Mark Wilkinson works naturally in wood, even when it comes to creating ways of drawing the huge curtains. In addition to the wooden pulley mechanism, this detail shows the wooden dowels that have been used to pin the whole structure together.

MEDIEVAL-STYLE HALL
LINED WITH MINSTRELS' GALLERIES

Mark Wilkinson started his working life as a furniture maker. His father is a carpenter, as was his grandfather. Wood is quite obviously in his blood—as familiar and reliable to him as dough would be to a third-generation baker.

Today Wilkinson makes sought-after wooden furniture and kitchens notable for his skilled use of hard wood—so it is entirely suitable that he should be living in a wood-framed house, part of which dates from 1420. The other, larger part is his own design and work which, by chance, was ready just before the celebrations marking the start of the third millennium. Many of the techniques used in its construction would have been familiar a thousand years earlier.

Although the new building is a modern construction that simply uses lumber in the age-old way, Wilkinson admits that it is inspired by the great soaring halls of medieval times rather than by barn architecture, which is why the necessary corridors and niches are, in fact, like open minstrels' galleries. The spaces may be as complex as the carpentery techniques their owner uses, but the building has a majestic simplicity because it draws on a tradition that has lasted a thousand years and still holds good.

The whole impressive space is made of huge pieces of green oak, beams as thick as 14 x 12 in (36 x 30 cm), which support some of the corridors, while others are cantilevered out from the walls of the earlier house, whose gray and worn timbers make up one entire wall of the hall and sitting room. The original house now consists of only two rooms—a kitchen on the ground floor and Mark's bedroom above it.

Since the whole area is open plan, there are plenty of angular, irregular spaces that can be put to good use. One space under the stairs has become an impromptu storage area for saddles and bridles; another houses a collection of ornate

BELOW The complex system of open galleries that lead from the stairs in the great hall to various bedrooms are cantilevered from the main walls. This reduces the hall's ceiling height from vast to something more modest.

ABOVE Corridors had not been invented in medieval times, and it was customary to walk through strangers' bedrooms. But Mark Wilkinson has created an ingenious system of wooden galleries around the walls of his great hall that allow access to all the upstairs rooms. Parts of the original 1420s' house are visible here, as are a later slated roof and square timbering.

OPPOSITE The old gray 15th-century oak timbers and beams of the early house contrast with the newer galleries and doors that link the two buildings. Wilkinson has made no attempt to disguise the seam between the two. The old building now comprises his own bedroom and, below, the kitchen.

Victorian oil lamps, while large bookcases—of solid wood, of course—form a working library in an upstairs corridor. "I got into wood because it is the stuff I use. I know the material, I understand it, it's my vocabulary. I thought a room of this size which wasn't timbered would seem alien. And I wanted a big room because I like space, you can take deep breaths in it. I always feel my shoulders are hunched in low rooms.

"Of course, this space needed corridors to get to all the other rooms, and I thought it was pointless boxing them up so I gave them lots of space so people can troll around on the galleries."

A large staircase rises straight from the hall up into the first collection of corridors on the second floor and from there, people can turn left along a gallery that leads to Mark's bedroom, with the kitchen door beneath; or right along another gallery, which houses the library. An opening in the wall leads to another set of smaller stairs that rise to a second floor. "From the top, you can look past the middle floor onto the ground floor—a nice, complicated view."

"Complicated" is the right word here. Wood-framing is a complicated business of angles, joints, wall plates, and supporting beams which, if correctly used, create splendid soaring spaces. Mark has taken full advantage of this, not only using medieval skills and techniques, but also marrying modern technology to the whole. Thus, all the floors on the three storys of rooms and corridors have underfloor heating, although all are of the traditional elm planks. These were imported from Michigan because elm is virtually unobtainable in Europe, even though it once grew there like a weed. "In

SINCE THE WHOLE AREA IS OPEN PLAN, THERE ARE PLENTY OF
ANGULAR, IRREGULAR SPACES THAT CAN BE PUT TO GOOD USE.

ABOVE The complex of wood-framed rooms, stairs, galleries, and landings combines to creater plenty of crannies for stowing interesting everyday objects. Here saddles, bridles, hard hats, and other riding impedimenta have been slung carelessly into the space under the stairs.

LEFT At the period when this house might have been built, England was covered in forests of hard wood, and wood was used to make everything. A corner of a landing shows how versatile a material wood can be in the hands of a master.

ABOVE CENTER Medieval buildings of this caliber were intended to be dramatic and imposing. Vast trees were felled to create the massive beams that hold up the entire structure—and the present owner has used oak tree trunks for the main floor-to-ceiling supports.

FAR RIGHT The scale of the wood-framed "extension" to Mark Wilkinson's original building means that the grand piano virtually disappears under the stairs. The gigantic and heavy curtains, which rise up the height of three storys, can be seen at the far end. Sensibly, Wilkinson has allowed the presence of the wood to speak for itself— very little color or pattern has been introduced into this enormous space.

wood-framed buildings, it was always oak for the beams and elm for the floor and so I had to get elm. Of course, it wasn't so difficult for me because I get shiploads of lumber. The firm in Michigan has some of the best ecological credentials of any I've dealt with."

The huge space is brilliantly light. There are large areas of glass on the roof that give interesting toplighting and a feeling of airiness. Complex angles and stairways are emphasized by light, too. The main room has a huge window—the sort that once might have been a gigantic door. "It's 18 feet high, running virtually from floor to ceiling. The curtains are massive; when you draw them, it feels like the theater and you expect organ music."

Mark Wilkinson feels strongly attuned to natural materials. Even the enormous boulder inset above the fireplace under one of the galleries has its own history. "On our farm there's a sandy ridge which was quarried for its sand. When they came across beds of stone, they simply dynamited it and discarded the rocks. They are just lying about in heaps. I scoop them up to use. This piece was about four feet thick, but we cut it down to about 18 inches deep and drilled it for steel bars and set it into concrete above the fire. I reckon it's probably nuclear-proof now."

Despite the drama of the wide spaces and heavy timbers, no tiny detail is ignored. The whole wall of the early house, including a layer of tiles, carefully adjoins the modern building in what Wilkinson hopes is a sensitive marriage; timbers are doweled, not nailed, and even the door latches and hinges are complicated machines made entirely of wood. Nothing, not the tiniest angle or space, is unconsidered in this extraordinary house.

LANDMARK
LOVINGLY RENOVATED

Olivia Douglas's grandparents lived in what has now become her own fabulous apartment on the tenth and eleventh floors of a landmark coop building in New York City. Her grandparents had originally purchased it in the 1940s, and Olivia, a real estate developer, bought it from their estate in 1988. She and her husband, David DiDomenico, have been its proud owners ever since.

The building was constructed in 1908 and, in Olivia and David's section at least, retained magnificent period features from that time, as well as what Olivia describes as a "very narrow and treacherous" set of stairs and halls: "We had to do a substantial renovation there."

According to their architects, CR Studio, "The new interior stitches together original details with the intervention of new materials, custom-designed furniture, and contemporary art work." To make it more fluid, the interior was stripped to its masonry shell before redesigning and redecoration began. The dark hall was lightened by the installation of a large new window, 6½ ft (2 m) tall, which faces east.

"The area on the second floor had been an office, leaving a space for the stairs that was only three feet wide," explains Olivia Douglas. "We converted this to a bathroom, which gave more space to the stairway, which is now six to seven feet wide. It lets the whole place breathe and feel better."

A wide hallway is now lined by a bookcase that stretches from floor to ceiling. It is a pleasant, light space where the owners can relax and flick through books while they decide what to read.

The end result of the conversion is a combination of the original period features with up-to-the-minute spaces. "We kept the architecture we liked, but spatially it's much more modern. We painted a wall bright yellow, and there's an orange doorway, an exit we don't use much. The functional spaces flow well—I think it works."

ABOVE Lining large corridors and landings with books and objects not only saves clutter elsewhere, but also insulates and softens the spaces.

MAIN PICTURE The splendid coop building had been little changed since the 1940s so the owners were able to retain all the interesting historic details, such as the classical fireplace, while updating areas that were dark or cramped. A new 6½ ft (2 m) tall window was essential—it made the apartment brilliantly light and friendly.

OPPOSITE, ABOVE LEFT The old staircase was ugly and treacherous, so it was replaced with one very much in keeping, but more generous and elegant. Much of the woodwork is left unpainted, from the floor to the banisters and stair treads.

OPPOSITE, BELOW LEFT The bookcases in the wide hall have been carefully designed so as not to detract from the historic elements of the two-story apartment. The area has been deliberately made light and airy to encourage browsing.

REVEALING THE HIDDEN DETAILS OF A
FINE RESTORATION

This splendid brownstone townhouse in New York was built in 1856 and—in common with nearly 80 percent of houses in the neighborhood—is considered an historic landmark building. This means that no element of the exterior can be changed without permission. There are no restrictions on what can be done to the interior, but the present owners bought the house with the intention of restoring and improving the entire five-story building.

At that time it consisted of a duplex on the fourth and fifth floors plus three rented apartments. "We wanted a family house for the four of us, not apartments," explains one of the owners, "so we gutted it and changed it into two sections." The ground floor is now an independent apartment, and the top four storys are lived in by the family. "The house is one of the tallest in the street and is also very wide for a brownstone."

Usually they are 20 ft (6 m) wide—this one is 25 ft (7.5 m). "We also opted for generous rooms—only two per floor plus bathrooms."

When they bought the house, all sorts of features were covered up. Guided by interior designer Gosia Rojek, the new owners set about uncovering the hidden details and, where bits were missing, carrying out restoration work.

"Everything was taken down, and the stairs were brought back to what they were originally. Layers and layers of paint were removed from the spindles on the staircase," says Gosia.

The result was extraordinary—many different exotic woods appeared from under the grime of centuries. The staircase treads—now unpainted—turned out to be pine; the banister rail was deep walnut; and the main post at the start of the banisters was rosewood. The spindles were mahogany. "Now it's cleaned up, it looks as

OPPOSITE This mid-19th-century townhouse, New York style, had fallen on hard times before being bought by the present owners who, with the help of designer Gosia Rojek, uncovered many original details that previous owners had covered up. At least they hadn't been ripped out when they were unfashionable.

ABOVE LEFT When they bought the venerable brownstone, it was divided into apartments (spoiling the grandeur of its entrance and stairs). Now the top four storys are reunited as a family house. It is the tallest in the street and built unusually wide, which gives huge scope for wide open spaces.

ABOVE Among the many original details revealed when coverings were removed was this fine, deep carving and imposing paneling on the inner entrance door. Paint has been removed to show off the rich mahogany to best advantage.

though everything had always been there, though much was painted from the start," says Gosia. "The entrance lobby is floored in oak with a cherry band; this was normal at the time the place was built. The entry door—covered under hundreds of layers of paint so you couldn't see any details—is pine. Leaving it just wood—and I love the warmth of wood—brings out the carved detail."

The entrance was also narrow and dark, so the interior designer removed the wall into the main second-floor room to make an arch, which leads directly into the living room. This arch was the copy of another on the same floor between the living room and dining room. "The entry had been very enclosed. You came in with walls on the right and stairs in front of you. It was dark and awful with dark green wallpaper. Now it feels very open—you almost walk straight into the living room with its marble fireplace." Right from the front

door, the walls are covered with pictures, and in the entrance is a huge mirror with a wood frame. A collection of antique Polish maps is displayed along the halls and up the stairs.

From all this you might imagine that the family lives in a traditional 19th-century brownstone. This is far from the case: where restoration was not involved, they opted for ultramodern objects. For example, the lights are by designers such as Achille Castiglione, and huge amounts of glass are incorporated in the interior, in everything from glass mosaic tiles to washbasins.

"We do have a lot of modern things, and it tends to shock visitors," says one of the family. "Though, within three minutes, they admit to liking what we've done. We wanted something different from the neighbors. We felt that, once you'd seen one of these buildings, you'd seen them all." Not in this case.

AS LAYERS AND
LAYERS OF PAINT
WERE REMOVED,
MANY DIFFERENT
EXOTIC WOODS
APPEARED FROM
UNDER THE GRIME
OF CENTURIES.

LEFT The brownstone's stairways are not only wide
and imposing, but show enormous care in the
detailing. Curves below the banisters are deeply
carved and rise up from the ground-floor stairs over
several storys. The wood used for the baseboards,
doors, and their frames has been uncovered.

ABOVE Even in less grand areas, when the scale
of the stairs diminishes, the quality of the carving
continues. Such careful work has been allowed
to remain both unadorned and uncluttered.

SANCTUARY FROM THE CITY AT A
WEEKEND ESCAPE

Weekend homes invariably have a different atmosphere from those we live in during the week. Weekdays mean work, stress, rush, and efficiency—we need to be somewhere with a washing machine, a freezer, a phone, a computer, a fax machine. Weekends are, ideally, for relaxation, slopping around, entertaining, and getting away from it all—to a place where no machines are needed to maintain the quality of daily life.

Nothing could exemplify the fantasy weekend home more vividly than this house belonging to a New York City designer and his partner, a director of Barneys store. This is an archetypal retreat from the most stressful city in the world. "We chose this area because it is only a short ferry crossing from Long Island, yet once you're on the boat you feel totally remote and cut off from things," says the designer. "The minute I'm on the water I feel like I'm on vacation—it acts like a moat, isolating us from our hectic lives. By the time we arrive on the island, we are effectively misanthropic shut-ins—to the extent that we become almost feral, barely even bothering to wash or get dressed. We cook, chill, frolic, and take dips on the deserted beach, and that's about it."

This is a wild exaggeration, of course. The pair use the word "feral" as a joke. "We would love to spend a month or so on the island—the most we ever manage is a couple of weeks—but I couldn't live there all year round. There's no culture for one thing, and when I say 'feral,' I don't mean that feral."

What they mean is that the house on Shelter Island, poised between the two busy forks of Long Island, is somewhere where appearances don't matter. The design of the house does, but their daily lives revolve around rest and recreation rather than work. The building,

OPPOSITE **This weekend retreat, on aptly named Shelter Island, set between the two forks of Long Island, is intended to free the owners from the busy, stressful life of New York. White is used throughout to augment the strong, clear light from the sea and the island, while a central woodburning stove adds warmth and comfort.**

ABOVE, LEFT **Many of the objects in the house, such as these flower-patterned pillows, have been chosen because they are handmade and naive, and come in simple designs.**

ABOVE **Water is the element in which this retreat wallows: the creek is a minute's walk away, and the owners are constantly taking to their kayak or running the dog beside the bay. So the plain tongue-and-groove quality of the building suits the maritime theme.**

WHITE IS LEAVENED ONLY BY SHADES OF GRAY—SO THE HALLS,
GALLERIES, AND OTHER CORNERS BECOME ONE OPEN SPACE.

probably always a hideaway, seems to have been built from a kit by an airline pilot around 1972 in a place that is refreshingly wholesome, they say, after the frenzy of the Hamptons.

They had been looking for a classic A-frame on Shelter Island for a couple of years before finding this one, which was perfect. "It was bright and upbeat—and the image of a groovy pilot living here brought to mind those great 1970s' Sunset books." Luckily, it had been little modified since that time, and they quickly covered any sins with a floor-to-ceiling coat of pure white paint. "White space is the perfect backdrop for lots of color," says the designer, who throws his own brilliantly colored pots in the garage alongside.

The unadorned white of the stairs, walls, rails, and furniture is leavened only by shades of gray—with the result that the halls, galleries, and other corners all combine in one open space. Originally the house had only a single spare bedroom along with the master bedroom in the attic, so an extension was added to provide another bedroom and bathroom—painted white, of course.

Even so, the focus of the whole house, and the only heat source, is a centrally placed black-iron stove. The presence of the stove—with its huge, angled, black metal chimney climbing up beside the white stairs—is made more impressive by the fact that it represents the only touch of black in the house. Even the fireplace, piled with pebbles found on nearby shores, is pure white, but then the details—tongue-and-groove walls, simple ladder-type stairs with no risers, chunky square-frame banisters—positively demand such treatment.

"It's a bit like a nunnery," one of the owners comments. "It's the most comfortable house you'll ever visit," say the architects, Schefer Design. The two descriptions are not incompatible.

OPPOSITE The owners of this classic A-frame house located only a few minutes' walk from the water covered everything with a coat of pure white paint. Then they stepped back a bit and added a few touches of light gray. When combined with the clear, seaside light, this subtle use of color emphasizes the interesting textures of the building.

ABOVE RIGHT Wood has been used decoratively throughout the seaside retreat. All the ceilings are fashioned from tongue-and-groove planks, and the banisters of the stairs are straightforward pieces of wood. But the decision to coat everything in white means that the angles and perspectives are emphasized.

RIGHT The same angle of the stairs viewed from a different perspective demonstrates the clever way in which the white-on-white effect of the banisters frames the view to the garden and the water beyond.

CAPTURING A LOOK THAT MEANS
CLASSY CASUAL

Stairs and landings are rarely comprehensively cluttered, and it is even rarer to find it done stylishly—but this house in upstate New York brings a new meaning to the phrase shabby chic. From the instant you step inside the front door, you are faced with the owner's pleasure in objects—how they are organized and displayed, how a piece with a specific use can be transformed into something of beauty. The mix is eclectic, but chosen with a unifying artistic eye.

Although some of the objects are chosen for enjoyment—the pair of ornate iron urns and the old metal letters from a shop display, for example—others have a use, even though their use may be subordinated to their appearance. The bulletin board holds a collection of scraps and clippings, but messages can be left on it, too; a basket of woven wooden slats has clothing for outdoors. The binoculars are used for spotting birds, and the

walking canes are kept handy for countryside treks. What draws the whole together is the insistence on a single dominant color— in this case, soft blue-gray. The chairs are painted in it, as is the basket; the round mirror above the urns has a blue-gray frame. Even the string bag has been dyed to match—the true stylist never ignores such apparently minor details—and even the leaves stuffed into a little bucket are a similar soft shade.

The same casual touch extends up the uncarpeted stairs into what was once no more than an empty light-filled landing. Here a welcoming daybed piled with pillows—blue-gray, of course—has been teamed with a desk of the same shade. There is a set of bookshelves, and instead of a painting, a blue and gray vintage dress hangs over a strip of grass matting.

There is nothing in this house that is of much intrinsic value—but all has great worth.

THIS PAGE AND OPPOSITE, ABOVE RIGHT Halls, entrances, and stairs need to look effective from different angles. The main picture shows the decorated entrance hall as seen by someone coming down the stairs and leaving the house. The urns are accentuated, as is the casual matting of the hall and the wide-open entrance door. When the same area is seen from floor level (opposite, above right), other elements of the design are developed. The mirror above the urns becomes more important, as does the rickety hall table with two drawers.

OPPOSITE, LEFT, AND BELOW RIGHT Landings do not need to be as formal as receiving rooms, but can still be functional. The owner of this retreat has created a daytime bedroom at the top of the stairs by positioning a daybed alongside two upper-floor windows. A closer look (opposite, below right) reveals how it has been made up of thrift-shop finds—a painted table, a camping chair, and an artfully positioned pair of slippers.

BELOW Photographers' homes always have a strong sense of space and drama—and that of Marie-Pierre Morel is no exception. Here she uses a blown-up portrait photograph casually propped on a table with a zebra skin below. The ladder and filing cabinet are both designed to give height and presence to a large space.

BOTTOM Marie-Pierre's professional assignments often take her to Africa, where she is an avid collector of tribal artefacts. Some typical shapes are arranged on a rustic table below the ladderlike staircase.

RIGHT Marie-Pierre's home has been developed from an old spring workshop in the center of Paris. The redesign of the interior artfully uses the space and height of the old industrial premises by doubling and reducing the ceiling height in separate areas.

MAIN PICTURE François Muracciole, the photographer's choice of architect, was briefed to create a comfortable living space in the former workshop that would not only incorporate practical working areas but also retain the feeling of an industrial space.

COSMOPOLITAN SETTING FOR A
FACTORY REFASHIONED

Marie-Pierre Morel is a professional photographer of house interiors around the world, so you would expect her own home to be full of interest. She lives in a former iron-spring factory in the Belleville and Republic areas of Paris—home, she says, to at least 50 different nationalities. "It's very popular, very mixed—not at all chic, but lively, cheap, and nice."

The "factory" is perhaps better described as an atelier, the base of a small private firm where craft and industry combined to create objects such as springs of high quality in small quantities—typical of the small industrial places that still abound in Paris. The atelier was producing goods up to six months before the time Marie-Pierre and her husband discovered the building for sale in 1997, and as a result, quite a lot of the fixtures and furniture have been salvaged from its wreck. With the architect François Muracciole, Marie-Pierre

spent six months creating her home from two storys of the space, located behind a small courtyard. She has lived there for four years and still loves her unconventional home.

"François was the friend of a friend, and I saw that he had done a nice project for that friend—a single room which was very clever and very simple. He had kept all the spirit of the house, and I thought he could make something clever and simple at the factory so that it would still remain the factory at heart."

This is surely the case. The spring factory seems almost untouched, with its series of metal-floored galleries, stacks of iron cupboards, now filled with rows of books, and heavy, old-fashioned iron radiators and banks of heavy metal hanging lights. The dark wooden floor is exactly the type which would have been installed early last century to cope with serious metalworking.

Using a combination of industrial metal floors found at the spring factory and Marie-Pierre's flea-market finds, Muracciole actually created these galleries, bookshelves, and stairs from scratch.

"We recycled a great deal from the factory, but the bookcases, for example, were inspired by a single small set of shelves I bought at a flea market," says Marie-Pierre. "They had come from a branch of the Banque de France. The ladder, which leads to the gallery, was designed by François."

The gallery is filled with quantities of books—the French are lucky in that their paperbacks come in standard sizes which gives a uniform impression—and with African sculpture and artefacts. Marie-Pierre's husband is a maker of documentary films who often visits the African continent, bringing back pieces from remote places. "I love objects and books, and therefore I have a lot of both. Both my husband and I travel a lot and bring things back."

Most of the furnishings, stationary or mobile, are in the kind of neutral shades you would expect in a factory. There is dull steel, dark wooden floors, and off-white walls. Even the furniture has been recycled from factories: in addition to the shelves from the bank, there's a pair of metal tables once used for sorting mail in post offices. Chairs, too, were found in flea markets and probably came from similar ateliers as the spring factory itself.

The final charming touch to this individual and chic hideaway in Paris's immigrant area is the way the huge plate-glass windows can be opened up on hot days, bringing the courtyard, planted with bamboo, into the main double-height room. There's even a tiny patio in the complex. This, of course, is far too industrial to be planted with blooming roses or geraniums. "I don't want flowers," says Marie-Pierre, with a shudder.

THIS PAGE The impression of a factory space has been encouraged by a combination of bargains from old-fashioned offices, modern industrial lighting, and the ladder that spans two floors. Examples of the lighting—designed especially for the apartment by Muracciole—can be seen attached to the ladder (this page) and hanging from the ceiling (right).

RIGHT A single, small set of shelves, originally installed in a branch of the Banque de France, was discovered and bought from a flea market by Marie-Pierre. The shelves inspired her and her architect to develop this impressive wall of books—proving that chance encounters can emerge as major factors in creating the design scheme for a whole apartment.

FIVE-STORY VICTORIAN
WITH A WEALTH OF ORIGINAL FEATURES

Jonathan Ross and his wife, Camilla, live in one of the busiest, most cosmopolitan roads in London, a main thoroughfare where the traffic never stops. Since this is also studio-apartment land, he believes that their house is one of the few that still exists undivided in the entire area. Indeed, it is an extraordinary survival in the setting.

The house was built in the grand style in 1872, and from 1914 until 1997 had been lived in by the same family. "Virtually all the original features were intact, although a bit of work had been done in the 1950s." It is enormous—about 5,000 sq ft (470 sq m) in total and, says Jonathan Ross, much less noisy than people might imagine. "It is set back from the road, and we tend to live towards the back of the house." The couple also uses the five storys for their work. Camilla is an artist

who has a studio in the building, while he runs a gallery from the house. This in effect reduces it to a two-bedroom house.

Having been clever enough to find this unrestored gem, the Rosses have taken immense care to conserve all its original features— from the fine encaustic tiles of terracotta, blue, yellow, and black that cover the floors of the entrance hall to the stone stairs leading from it, which have been painstakingly stripped of ancient paintwork to reveal a pale gray natural finish. The stairs leading down to the basement have been painted to match.

Although at first sight the restoration has modern touches— such as the rope banister flanking the stairs to the basement gallery and the sisal matting covering the stairs themselves— Jonathan Ross points out that both features were used in

FAR LEFT Never get rid of original features in a house without a great deal of thought. The combination of the etched glass in the entrance door and the colorful encaustic tiles so popular in Victorian times makes this hall unforgettable.

THIS PAGE AND INSET, LEFT This style cannot be achieved by fakery. It depends on original features. For example, the heaviness of the mahogany handrail could not be reproduced today, when old mahogany is virtually impossible to find, and although encaustic tiles do turn up in salvage yards, this quantity would be hard to come by in an unspoiled state. The stone stairs are very unusual.

ABOVE AND BELOW LEFT An early 19th-century folding table, with welcoming flowers, stands in front of the glazed screen flanking the basement stairs. The stairs descend from the hall to the art gallery—a space that once accommodated kitchens, sculleries, and servants' rooms. The screen of glass was always there, but it was opaque, which the Rosses replaced. They also put in the rope to help people going downstairs.

OPPOSITE AND BELOW RIGHT Among the ranks of books that occupy the landing library are old

photographs and objects and—especially interesting and totally in keeping with the date of the house—Jonathan Ross's collection of 19th-century stereoscopic viewers and stereographoscopes. They resemble sophisticated binoculars, but are intended to turn old photographs into 3D images or enlarge them. There are also viewers and lenses for scrutinizing details in early pictures. Ross is clearly fascinated by photographic tricks and treats, for his gallery specializes in modern holograms, three-dimensional art that uses light to achieve its effects.

the 19th century. He prefers the restoration to be described as a Victorian interior reworked with a modern eye, with the emphasis on conservation.

The newest features of all are the halogen downlighters and modern hanging lanterns, which brighten up the hall when the door is closed. The generous dimensions of the stairs and corridors have made it possible to furnish them fully. The main corridor, leading from the front door, has a lobby and original inner door of frosted, etched glass that provides both light and privacy. A 19th-century folding table stands in front of the glass screen separating the hall from the basement stairs, which descend to what is now an art gallery. The original screen was made of opaque glass, which has now been replaced.

The stairs leading up are immensely grand, with ornate iron balusters and a heavily carved mahogany handrail. On the other side, most of the early Anaglypta relief paper on the walls was intact; the Rosses simply left the gaps and other damage as they were and painted over the whole lot in soft gray copied from an old Swedish house.

Even cleverer was their idea to paint the walls above the dado scumbled yellow, which imperceptibly lightens as you go up. "It's warm and welcoming when you arrive and gradually gets cooler as you go up, to make you feel lighter."

One generous landing has become a library. "The way the main rooms are made, with flush walls on either side of the fire, means that the normal place for bookshelves doesn't exist. The landing is quite wide enough for books. There was a bathroom there, put in sideways, and we ripped it out. It's a bright spot, and we browse through books around there."

There are plenty of late 19th-century houses in London with many original features still intact (or, as in the Rosses' house, hidden under hideous carpeting). Those who are lucky enough to have the wide spaces typical of the period, the high ceilings, the generous detailing, and the careful attention to banisters, stair risers, and ceiling moldings can take a leaf from the Rosses' example. Their reworking of halls and landings has hardly deviated from the authentic yet, in their careful coloring, use of lighting, and lack of clutter, the areas seem thoroughly modern. For example, the basement, so ideal for a gallery, would be equally useful for a children's playroom or an office, and the landing bookshelves could be transformed into spaces for attractive collections.

BELOW In a truly small space, it is an effective strategy always to emphasize the natural available light and the views from the windows—both of which encourage a sensation of space and exterior vistas. The artfully arranged mirrors and paintings in this apartment draw the attention by degrees toward the open window.

RIGHT Much ingenuity has been used in this small New York space to house office equipment that can be hidden after hours. A series of floor-to-ceiling screens can be pulled into place to conceal the working areas. The fact

that they are plain and used throughout makes them blend in with the ordinary walls.

OPPOSITE, ABOVE The owner specializes in matching people in need of design skills with appropriate designers. As such, her small apartment must demonstrate her use of art and technology at its best.

OPPOSITE, BELOW One thing all owners of tiny apartments have to learn is how to combine practical areas with stylish design. In this example, the working kitchen is also home to chic modern lighting and an overscaled mirror.

A DESIGNER'S
HOME OFFICE

When an apartment is as compact as Karen Fisher's, every single bit of space must work for itself. It is only 500 sq ft (45 sq m) in floor area, but with the advantage of a terrace overlooking a New York City park. "There is light on all sides—but no room," she says. "Yet I work, entertain, eat, and sleep here."

Karen Fisher founded and continues to run Designer Previews, a service that matches international designers with those who want to use their skills. Clients come to her office, adjoining the apartment, to choose from an enormous range of decorating styles, from English country to Oriental. She is therefore perfectly placed to find a designer suited to her own needs.

The small apartment has been designed by Clodagh, who first worked on it seven years ago. Clodagh's challenge was to find space where none existed and to turn the limited space into a working area. Great ingenuity was used to hide office equipment and cupboards behind all-concealing panels, and to make built-in furniture that could be packed away when not needed or used for more than one purpose—one bookcase converts into a table, for example.

Clodagh first painted the apartment strong burnt sienna, but recently Karen wanted a change. "I gave her a different mandate. I changed over those seven years: I began to yearn for simple elegance and serenity; a more neutral palette. And I desperately wanted more light."

The space is now completely transformed. Clodagh used layer upon layer of Venetian stucco—a traditional plaster mixed with paint—to color the entire area in soft taupe that changes tones as the light moves around. The centuries-old technique has another benefit—the surfaces are never bland but show evidence of the many layers involved. Does it work? Perfectly.

LEFT Their first sight of its stupendous entrance hall and staircase persuaded the present owners of this English country house to buy. Designed in 1937, the house was the height of modernity at the time—and even today, more than six decades later, it has a sharpness and simplicity that draws gasps from visitors.

BELOW Fortunately, much of the original hall and stairs, designed by Raymond McGrath, had been retained by previous owners of the house. The style of the interior is reminiscent of the magnificent cinemas of the period—Hollywood's finest years—though sensitively rescaled to meet the demands of domestic living.

ROUND HOUSE
THAT IS NOW AN ICON OF MODERNISM

Not many people can claim that the entrance hall and stairs sold them an entire property, but the couple who bought this house can—and do. They heard by chance that an extraordinary Modernist creation in an 18th-century park in Surrey was for sale. Designed in the International Style by Raymond McGrath in 1937, it is thought to be the very first shuttered and poured-concrete house in Britain. The shuttering was made of Oregon pine, whose strong grain still imprints the exterior of this circular, drum-shaped house.

"The entrance immediately sold it to us," one of the owners told me. "We opened the big, curved door to a feeling of space and light to see the staircase curving upward. It's breathtakingly beautiful. We fell in love with it immediately, and it's still a thrill to walk in. There's a wall of mirrors and, in mosaic mirror tiles, a map of the house as McGrath designed it." The garden was designed by Christopher Tunnard, who published his book *Gardens in the Modern Landscape* in 1938. The family had, almost unwittingly, bought a house that was famous in Modernist circles. The first weekend after they arrived, a whole coachload of Dutch architects turned up to have a look.

"We've always loved Modernist houses, but we didn't know much about them. We were sent details and thought the house looked interesting, though it was miles from where we wanted to live. When we saw it, it was full of ruffles and wallpaper, and we had to strip it back to its Modernist past, with white walls, bare windowsills, all a bit minimalist. We felt the previous owners had confused Modernism with Art Deco, and we didn't think that was right. We wanted the building to be white everywhere, cool, quiet, and peaceful."

The couple's three sons live at the top of the house, in an area of their own up the curving staircase, and this allows the rest of the space, which is curvaceous and near open-plan, to be utterly disciplined. There is no clutter

THIS PAGE Wallpaper and ruffles had been used to cover the lines of this fine entrance, but have now been stripped back by the current owners. The whole area is floored in terrazzo, and heating elements have been installed underneath. A simple glass hanging light solves the problem of how to combine modern lighting with such a strong statement.

LEFT AND ABOVE The terrazzo floors
have been laid in large tiles, which
are curved to suit the drum shape
of the entire building. The stairs with
their blond wood banister rail follow
the same sweep. These, along with the
small detailing at the start of each stair
riser, form the entire decoration of the
area. It needs no more.

or extraneous ornament. But the extremely strong character of the architecture has impressed the children. "They do appreciate living here," says their mother. "In Lanzarote we went to see a house carved from lava. It was very similar—and the boys said it was just like home."

McGrath used what was then the latest technology to build the house. It has stood the test of time. Much of the heating, especially in the halls, is under the floors, beneath the terrazzo tiles that cover both hall and stairs. Elsewhere, radiators are built into the walls and almost hidden. The wood used everywhere in the house, providing virtually the only color apart from white, is generally exotic—maple, ash, and African walnut. Not only the stairs, but also the banisters curve in a most sexy

manner. The horizontals are painted soft off-white and held in place by steel supports. The handrail is of blond wood. When restoration work was under way, it took one of the builders a week with an emery board to get it back to its original shade, many tones lighter than it had become.

Soon after buying this famous house, the couple realized that it had declined into decrepitude and needed serious restoration to recapture its architectural purity.

"The walls were in a bad state, the house was tired and run down, and the grounds were a jungle. It was frightening." Far more so, I imagine, than taking on a normal brick or wood house, for they were up against revolutionary building techniques. They hired the architects Munkenbeck & Marshall

RIGHT As the stairs snake upward, their curves emphasized by the wood banister rail with three horizontal metal rails underneath, the ceilings follow the line. The pure white walls are left severely unadorned. During daytime hours, natural light floods through the extensive areas of glass found in this part of the building—its effect enhanced by the austere whiteness of the walls.

BELOW A vase of white lilies is set against one of the most interesting features of McGrath's interior: a mosaic mirror etched with a map of the property. It was this area of entrance hall and stairs that "sold" the house to the owners, and they have been able to keep the space both spare and welcoming.

to oversee the house's re-creation. Everything was restored to the original, in accordance with the mosaic map in the entrance hall. The result is spectacular. Since the whole is circular, everything–from the staircase to the walls and the front door–curves. The building also has a central point from which every detail radiates, not only the internal block floors, but also those outside. Many of the walls are actually windows and–since the building is on an escarpment–light floods in throughout the day. The interior walls are of typically Modernist translucent glass bricks and these, too, encourage luminosity.

Large rooms open off the staircase. A south-facing living room with 12 large windows overlooks a terrace and the garden beyond. The kitchen has a curved partition wall of wood and ribbed glass, and a central working block with black marble tops. On the floor above, the main bedroom sits on top of the living room, again with a dozen large windows and even more spectacular views. You can step out from here onto a wisteria-covered balcony as though in a Le Corbusier house in the Mediterranean.

If the present owners knew little about Modernist style when they bought their house, their knowledge has since increased immensely. They have become enveloped in its style and beauty, and now feel more like custodians than owners. Another coachload of Dutch architects would be even more welcome today than they were four years ago, for the family loves showing off its spectacular home.

LEFT **The entire house is based on a drum shape that is carefully followed through in the interior, meticulously designed by the architect in 1937. This part of the main hall contains not only the mosaic glass showing a map of the property but also another wall covered in sheer mirror glass. The beams and floor tiles follow the curves.**

RIGHT **Thirties' style made much of mirrors, sheet glass, opaques, and translucents. Semitranslucent glass bricks have been used to create an interior curved corridor that allows a distant glimpse of the outside world through a transparent glass window.**

SINCE THE WHOLE BUILDING

THIS PAGE As a contrast with the glass bricks used as windows (left), the floor-to-ceiling walls of the kitchen area have been made entirely of glass bricks. The massive dividers create an impression of niches set within the curve. The owners have highlighted this effect by placing a modernist stool within each bay.

IS CIRCULAR, EVERYTHING—FROM STAIRS TO WALLS—CURVES.

RIGHT Clever designers use existing features to stylish advantage. In this case, the broad floorboards of the original building have been left alone to gleam with the light coming through a distant window. The modernist chair is placed so its silhouette is always visible.

BELOW Virtually all necessities have been hidden from sight in cabinets with sliding doors and no handles, making them meld with the walls.

PARKSIDE APARTMENT THAT SPELLS
SERENE BELGIAN

Some of the most interesting of the unconsidered spaces in apartments and houses are those created by owners who are also architects or designers. Such is the case with this serene apartment in Antwerp belonging to the designer Claire Bataille and her husband, Yves Borin.

Claire formed a design partnership in 1968 with Paul ibens, and the duo worked together on the Antwerp apartment over many years. Writing in the magazine *Domus*, Marco Romanelli was wildly enthusiastic about the clarity and "paradigmatic quality" of the design. While I am not quite sure what this means—paradigm is one of those fashionable words that are hard to define—I do know that Romanelli loved its calm functionality and simplicity. Simplicity is, of course, extremely hard to achieve in a smallish space.

The apartment is on the best floor of an apartment building with a fine view over King Albert Park from the front and its own garden at the back. Although the building dates from the 19th century, each floor was made into an apartment in the 1920s. Claire Bataille bought hers in the 1960s and has changed it several times since. The most recent and drastic alterations were carried out by her and Paul ibens in 1992.

Like most of these apartments, it consisted of three main rooms linked by doors, and the central room got little light. Now the spaces have been opened up so that, as soon as you arrive in the main area—through the entrance door and up a set of narrow stairs—you see rooms in both directions and, through the windows, the park in front and the garden at the rear. The dining room has a sliding glass door that is almost always left open.

LEFT The owners lived in the Antwerp apartment for about 30 years before, in 1992, they opened up the spaces so that light from the main rooms flooded into central, previously darker areas. The dining room's glazed and sanded gliding doors are invariably left open. This room, unlike the rest of the place, has a wall of anthracite stucco.

THIS PAGE The empty hallway conceals a powder room and coat-hanging space for guests. The whole set of rooms, apart from two walls in both living room and dining room, are painted white and have lofty ceilings. The furniture and pictures are unthreatening in style, but the way they have been placed contributes to the severity of the scheme.

LEFT The entrance lobby is set up exactly as such an area should be—featuring a large old-fashioned hall stand full of umbrellas, oversized walking canes for leisurely strolls over the nearby cliffs, hats and coats bleached by sea winds, and binoculars to spot migrating birds. A small side table is covered with old embroidered tray cloths and lace.

OPPOSITE AND BELOW LEFT From the entrance lobby, the stairs go up to a bedroom floor, hung with a flowery antique quilt—but, more curiously, they also go down to the main hall of the house. The quilt has been used here not only to give extra visual interest to the plain banisters of the wide stairs, but also to screen off a small sitting area with its comfy woven arm chair. At every level, the owner has introduced small tables, each decorated with a simple bunch of country flowers. These surfaces are also a practical way of holding objects in transit—as anyone with a multistoryed house will be quick to appreciate.

ISLAND IDYLL
WITH SCOTTISH ECHOES

Clara Baillie is a Scot who has settled about as far from her home territory as is possible in Britain. Her house is on the Isle of Wight, a short ferry ride from England's southern coast. But she has managed to find a home redolent of the mountains and glens. It is just like a Scottish shooting lodge, built around 1810 of old gray stone, rambling and welcoming. The strange configuration of the Isle of Wight house encourages informality, and its slight eccentricity recalls those northern shooting lodges which, as like as not, were designed by laird, factor, and builder without the smell of an architect.

Entrances are always important in a house, but this fact often goes unrecognized. The Baillies' house is entered through a glass-paned, arched door that is actually on a mezzanine level. Today, the door is constructed in a series of square panes that admit light. Mrs. Baillie thinks it was put in during the 1960s, when planning controls were less stringent. From the mezzanine, stairs lead up to the bedrooms and down to the house's main hall, which is dominated by a marble fireplace.

"It's a wonderful hall," Clara Baillie enthuses. "When we found the house eight years ago, we just fell in love with it. It was very dilapidated, but we could see how it could be." The whole space of the three-floored hallway is extremely generous and culminates in a coved ceiling, which may once have held a skylight. "It's really high, with a chandelier hanging from the arched ceiling. We have to put up scaffolding to paint it. When we bought the house, it was covered in relief paper, which I thought would never come off. The doors had all been painted with a wood grain. When we repainted the doors, it gave it a

THIS PAGE Fireplaces in foyers and on landings are not at all common, but where they are found they create a point of assembly for families and friends. The owners have taken advantage of this good-looking fireplace to add a woodburning stove, which can be closed and damped down in off-periods or opened up to welcome parties coming in from the wind. Pillows have thoughtfully been added.

huge lift." Since the sea is so close to the house, Clara Baillie has chosen a color scheme that relies on seawashed shades. "There is wonderful light on the island and the seaside influence here is very strong. So our colors tend to be turquoise, pale blue, and green. We've used Kelly's Taupe from Kelly Hoppen's line, along with a Laura Ashley blue on the ceiling and Laura Ashley's Coconut on the woodwork. We wanted it to be subtle and pale because it would be quite dark otherwise—especially the corridors that lead off the hall." The good pine floors have all been sanded and waxed, and being given only a few rugs adds to the welcoming atmosphere.

Although the building feels Scottish in inspiration, the setting is more typical of the Mediterranean coast. "The view from the house could be of the Mediterranean. We can see a vast expanse of sea—all the way to France—over the slate roofs of other houses. The island also has its own microclimate and is almost subtropical. The botanic gardens can grow things much better than Kew. I had never been here before we found the house, but my husband went to school at Bembridge, on the island, so he knew it well."

In summer, the 3 acres of garden and woodland reached through the glazed front door include tender Australian tree ferns, with olive trees, lemons, and a Natal sour plum in pots on the terrace. In winter they are moved into the conservatory. There is also a mimosa tree in the garden sheltered by huge holm oaks, which surround it.

ABOVE LEFT In a convenient space on the landing where the stairs descend from the front-door lobby and then continue down from the fireplace hall into the cellar, an old church pew has been padded with a plaid-covered seat and pillows—making an ideal place to curl up.

ABOVE AND BELOW Almost entirely as a result of the arrangement of the stairs, landings, halls, and corridors that were built into it, the whole place exudes relaxation and a casual approach to life. Other rooms are just as friendly, but the halls and stairs make an immediate impact on visitors.

FLAMBOYANT DISPLAY IN A
LUXURIOUS LOBBY

ABOVE Lithographs by Odilon Redon are hung, equally spaced, in two rows on the walls of the oversized lobby at the entrance to this apartment. The walls are painted cool dark red. The strength of the paintwork is counterbalanced by a check carpet in pale celadon gray that is similar to the mats. A white-painted dado around the hall also serves to reduce the quantity of red.

ABOVE RIGHT AND RIGHT The challenge for the designer of this spacious hallway was to find a way to unify the differently sized lithographs. Her answer was to put each into two different mats within uniform frames. An off-white mat sits next to each print (on paler paper still) and outside that is a pale gray mat. The frames she chose were delicate silver gilt.

OPPOSITE Marina was determined that the use of gilt—in paintwork, furniture, and frames—should be kept to a minimum. She used gilded silver on the frames along with furniture of brushed steel. The final touch is the elegant sofa—amazingly, a flea-market find—which has been covered in a reproduction 18th-century toile de Jouy that picks up the exact shades of the walls and woodwork.

Marina Killery is an interior designer and art adviser who specializes in finding pictures for her clients and then hanging and arranging the decor around them. She was therefore ideally suited to the role of organizing a large, sixth-floor apartment for a long-time friend who collects German Expressionist and Russian Avant-Garde pictures. She considered the decor of the rooms as she first saw them—especially the hall—entirely unsuited to such a modern collection. "It was extremely fussy, like Versailles. There was complete discord between the decor and the paintings. I set about redesigning it. Everything came out, everything was changed."

"I don't think the previous designer had understood his client, but then I was privileged to know him personally, and I knew his art collection." She believes that, even if clients do not know what they want, it is possible to lead them to discover their preferences by getting a sense of their likes and dislikes, even in something as simple as clothes.

So they went together to a print fair and bought a series of 24 lithographs of "The Temptation of St. Anthony" by Odilon Redon. They were all intended to be hung in the oversized hall at the apartment's entrance. "I love Redon. He is a master of lithography. He creates deep, velvety blacks with a resonance and depth no other black can have."

The whole space of the hall now proclaims the influences that have shaped the owner's design preferences. It is luxurious and welcoming; it is hung with an important series of lithographs exactly to the owner's taste. It is clearly masculine, and there is just a touch of "gentleman's club" about it.

PERIOD ELEGANCE
IN AN ADAPTABLE ENTRANCE HALL

TOP, ABOVE AND ABOVE RIGHT If London's planning regulations allowed it, many an owner of an 18th-century house would demolish the wall that divides the front entrance hall from the ground floor fronting onto the street (where the dining room was often located). Jane Churchill was lucky in that this had already been done in her house. As dining rooms are in less regular use today, she has been able to increase the light in the entrance corridor vastly—and to increase its apparent space—as well as allow the stairs to spring from a single square room.

OPPOSITE Since the whole ground floor entrance has been transformed by the removal of a wall, Jane Churchill can now treat the space as a grand entrance. It incorporates a large classical fireplace—with the fire lit in welcome—and the alcoves on either side are used to store books.

The best interior designers are both clever and opinionated, and Jane Churchill scores high on both counts. Her spatial skills and strong views have been used to particularly inspirational effect in the design and furnishing of the halls and landings of her London house.

Jane Churchill's starting point was the elegance common to period London houses, where detailing in the entrances and stairs is never skimped. The banisters always curve gracefully; the moldings in the corridors are as classical as those in the rooms; and the doors are paneled in good proportions.

The designer has used these built-in features to make a substantial room from the typical narrow hallway that normally leads to the stairs. She had a bit of luck in that, when she found the house, the wall dividing the front ground-floor room from the narrow hall had already been partly demolished. Today, this would probably not be allowed. "It was lucky because I cannot bear narrow passages—hate them. Now I can use the hall as a room, which is a great luxury."

Indeed, she does not use the hall as a hall at all. It is a combination of library, living room, and dining room—changing its character according to how the furniture is placed and how the central round table is laid.

In normal mode, the Regency loo table of exotic grained wood is piled with books, perhaps accompanied by a dramatic flower arrangement. It stands before an even more ornate chimneypiece with classical columns and broken pediments. The grate is filled with a natural-gas-fueled log fire, which is lit in cold weather. On either side of the fireplace large bookcases have been built in the alcoves, and these are completely filled with books.

LEFT When space is at a premium, it makes sense to put halls and corridors to multiple use. Jane Churchill has doubled the performance of the new, enlarged room by making it a library by day. Alcoves are filled with books, and a round table, set on a circular carpet, piled with magazines. By night or at lunchtime, the magazines are removed, and the round table is converted for eating with the addition of a lacy cloth and upholstered dining chairs. Up to 12 people can sit around it.

OPPOSITE, LEFT The hall is transformed by using tableware, glasses, and even flowers that complement the room's colors. When the table is set, the room appears to have been designed for eating alone. The hefty vase of imposing sunflowers seen among books on page 91 has been replaced by a smaller, prettier arrangement that picks up the blues of the glasses, chairs, and stairs beyond.

OPPOSITE, RIGHT The wall between the original narrow entrance corridor and what was once the ground-floor salon or dining room has not been demolished entirely. The large, square archway created between the two spaces means that they remain separate, but each gains light and airiness from the other.

BANISTERS ALWAYS CURVE GRACEFULLY, CORRIDORS HAVE CLASSICAL CORNICES, DOOR PANELS ARE WELL PROPORTIONED.

The problem of awkward proportions that arises when walls are knocked down—especially in these carefully arranged townhouses—has been cleverly concealed through the designer's skill.

First, not all the wall has gone. Instead, an opening like those in the second-floor rooms means that the room seems to include the extra space within the corridor area, although the corridor is not exactly part of it. The round table is positioned in the center of the old room, leaving the corridor clear. A grand console table sits against the corridor wall, with ornate candelabra on it and watercolors symmetrically grouped on the wall behind.

Under the round table, a circular rug emphasizes the spacing. "I collect round rugs. This is an Aubusson that has been cut up, and I have the middle bit—they were never made like that. It would be so boring if it was square." The floor under the rug, and in the corridor, too, has been stenciled in an

all-over pattern inspired by a Swedish design, which unites the entire space. The furniture is of the grandest: a pair of statuary "blackamoors" stand beside the fire, above which is a part-painted mirror. Blue-and-white Chinese vases are on brackets, while, further up the stairs, blue-and-white European plates are hung. The designer has also furnished the landings with panache. On one console table, a marble bust is flanked by plants in cachepots with botanical pictures ranged behind.

The overall grandeur of the setting makes the transition into a dining room for entertaining easy to achieve. The stacks of books are whisked off the table and replaced by a large white cloth that falls to floor level. Matched upholstered dining chairs appear, as do blue glasses and smaller arrangements of flowers. "Dining rooms are such a waste," she says firmly. "I can seat ten or twelve people here."

HOME DESIGNED AROUND A
BOOK SPACE

You might expect a family with the name of Foyle to have quite a few books, but Christopher and Catherine Foyle between them own thousands—he is the chairman and managing director of the renowned Foyles bookshop in London's Charing Cross Road, and is used to having stacks of them around the place. But he wanted something more—a modern version of a proper galleried library.

"This place is the fulfillment of a dream for Christopher," says Catherine of their stunning home in London's Notting Hill. "A long time ago, before we were married, he once saw a house that he longed to buy but couldn't afford, and it had a two-story library with books from floor to ceiling and a gallery all around. Seven years ago, he said to me, 'Why don't you spend the next couple of years looking for a place where I could re-create a room like that?' The next day I phoned Christopher and said, 'I've found it.'"

The building that fulfilled the fantasy is an old telephone exchange that had been subdivided by a developer into units for apartments. Peter Jones of Jones Lambell Architecture and Design, whose job it was to realize Christopher's dream, explains that the Foyles bought two units, one large area on the second floor and another one below it. The building was put up in the 1920s and could not have been better suited to the dozens of yards of bookshelves (and the corresponding weight of books) that would be housed there. "The building was designed to carry the heavy items used in historic telephone exchanges—transistors and electric devices. It was, technically, an industrial building of reinforced steel, so it was ideal. Weight was not a significant problem. The removal of a floor was."

The architects and their clients decided to take out a floor between the two apartments and restructure the roof space to create, in total, a three-story home. The semicircular end of the building was chosen as the place for a curved gallery that would take in two storys at double height. "At its highest, the room is

OPPOSITE **You would never guess that this combination of library and country-house-style living room is housed inside an old telephone exchange in London's chic Notting Hill district. But it was the sheer space needed by the old equipment that made the conversion possible.**

ABOVE **A twisting, freestanding staircase twines up from the ground-floor hall, just outside the main living room, to the book-lined gallery on** the second floor. A Regency loo table and upholstered armchair have been chosen to accentuate the curve of the stairs.

BELOW **When the stairs arrive at the gallery level, there is a choice between browsing among the book stacks or eating at the metal-footed dining table. The simplicity of the table and the metal cross-bars tie in with both the metal screens of the stairs and the gallery rails.**

33 feet up to the apex of the roof. A chimney goes right through the three-story space, up from the living room and gallery into the roof space." The home is, therefore, split level, with a foyer and living room on the first level and the gallery, kitchen, and a bedroom on the next floor. On the next floor up, there is another living room and a bedroom for one of the Foyles' daughters, Chrissie.

More unusually for this fashionable part of London, the building is a haven of privacy and peace. Outside, there is a countrified cobblestoned courtyard leading through a door onto a spiral staircase which, in turn, leads to a further door. Behind this is a warmly glowing hall, a cabinet to house Christopher Foyle's collection of writing boxes and slopes.

Philip Hooper, who worked with Jones Lambell on the interior, was given the chance to create everything from scratch. "We did keep the exterior windows for the facade," says Jones. "The interior windows were double-glazed and, to restrain the entire end of the building, we put in a new steel ring beam." The bookcases are cunningly designed to hide this beam. "The gallery provides structural support." The gallery on the upper of the two ground floors is cantilevered from the wall and has a beautiful steel and translucent glass walkway in front of each of the bookshelves. It is reached by a set of pale, curved, French limestone steps and encircled by an elegant bronze rail. There are wall lamps at strategic intervals between the stacks of books, and each window has a squab cushion for

OPPOSITE Many classical features have been deliberately added to the building's interior—despite the fact that it was originally designed for heavy industrial use. As the staircase arrives at the second floor, an *oeil de boeuf* window borrows light from the main gallery and provides a useful space for a Chinese baluster vase. The purpose of this small walled area is to add to the surprise and drama of the gallery itself.

THIS PAGE A major inspiration for this sensational curving gallery with its fine metalwork balustrade is the old British Museum Reading Room. The telephone exchange building was shaped like a prow at one end, and this was incorporated into the main curve. Windows, themselves arched, are set regularly between each cherrywood book stack with, below, a handy stuffed window seat. Each has its own angled lamp for nighttime browsing.

Unlike European apartment buildings, those in New York may be built without any interior stairs between floors (except those needed for fire escapes). Apartment buildings can simply rely on elevators to link the different floors. So, when the owners of one fourth-floor apartment decided to increase their space by buying the one below, the crucial question was where the stairs should be put and what they should look like.

There was no natural space for stairs, nor had the rooms been designed with a staircase and landing in mind. Therefore, combining the various rooms on the two floors required a complete overhaul of both apartments—so the family had to move out for six months.

Louise Harpman of the architect Specht Harpman says that to transform the two apartments, each consisting of five-and-a-half rooms, into a duplex was a complex process. It involved the design and construction of not only a new staircase, but also a new kitchen and informal dining room, a new hall to connect the entrance to the informal dining area, and a new master bedroom and bathroom. The architects also opened up the wall between the living room and dining room and installed new fixtures and finishes throughout.

"The relocation of the kitchen and introduction of an informal dining room at the rear led us to design a hallway articulated with lighted cabinets," explains Louise Harpman, "in part to showcase the owners' collection of Russel Wright pottery, while also creating an inviting promenade."

One of the owners, the creative director of a company that designs sweaters, seems to have enjoyed the whole experience. "We spent six months thinking about where the staircase should go. Eventually, the only solution was to open it

THE STAIRCASE IS A WORK OF ART IN ITSELF, WITH A DESIGN PRESENCE THAT MAKES IT THE FOCAL POINT OF THE HOME.

ABOVE While the lower of the two apartments basically holds the grander receiving rooms and adult areas, at the top of the new stairs there's a playroom for the owners' young children, plus play space for a large dog. A gate keeps the children safe from the stairs while letting their parents monitor what's happening above.

LEFT The architects designed the stairs to link the whole duplex, using wood for the stairs themselves and steel for the handrail. The design was inspired by the owners' collection of modern furniture.

OPPOSITE The simplicity of the lower floor's informal dining room is characteristic of the entire duplex, which originally consisted of five-and-a-half rooms per apartment. The owners are enthusiastic about mid-20th-century furniture and works of art, and use them with little added ornament. The harmony between architects and owners in this conversion has produced a stunning statement of 21st-century simplicity at its best.

up. My personal passion is 1950s Modern, so we went about the alterations from that standpoint. Louise Harpman and I hunted around for a design for the stairs and came up with a mid-century design that we spotted in the Seagram townhouse. It was so extreme that we couldn't do it exactly. But it was the inspiration for the openness of our stairs."

"It was a process of throwing ideas around until we got it—it was great. We gave the stairs a rail like a steamship." Louise Harpman explains how it was done: "The stairs join the public social spaces on the lower floors with the private family spaces above. The adult living room at the base of the stairs is linked to the children's playroom at the top of the stairs . . . This led us to design the wood stairs and steel handrail to facilitate spatial connection. Specht Harpman is known for clean, modern design, and the owners' interests were well matched with our own. The owner's interest in classic modern furniture, design objects, and features meshed with our own desire to retain the well-proportioned rooms already in place, while introducing a new vocabulary."

The success of the conversion centered on the stairs. The lower of the two floors became an open-plan loftlike space for living and dining, with the stairs rising to the playroom for the two children, aged two and four, and a large dog. There are also four bedrooms and two bathrooms.

Everywhere there are paintings to be seen—again, mid-20th-century Modern in style—along with the period furniture, which complements the apparent simplicity of the architecture. Indeed, the staircase is a work of art in itself, effortlessly sleek, luxuriously plain, but with the strong design presence necessary to make it the focal point of the home. And how does it feel now? "I adore it, it's wonderful," says the owner. "It's like having a house in New York City." Even the dog is happy.

THE
ELEMENTS

THE ELEMENTS

Since starting to write this book, I have been surprised by the number of people who have told me about their enthusiasm for what are generally thought of as unconsidered spaces.

No longer treated with dismissiveness, these areas of the home are apparently where architects, designers, and owners like to show off. Since halls and staircases do not, in theory, need to be relaxing or cozy—nor provide, for example, pools of light to work by—you can treat them with pizzazz. And people do. The high walls of even the smallest staircase and the extended length of corridors at the top of them are invitations to display collections. These can be great banks of pictures, either massed in sets (I have no fewer than 18 colored etchings of the Crimea up one wall, all framed in the same way and close-hung) or arranged in groups. These can be black-and-white or monochrome groups, those with a common

theme—animals, food, portraits—or with a common style such as that shared by the most influential English artists of the mid-20th century, Edward Bawden, Paul Nash, and Ben Nicholson.

Staircases can also be hung with textiles such as kimonos, tapestries, or African kente cloths, while corridors are perfect locations for custom-made shelves for books, groups of fossils, or Staffordshire pottery.

As long as these areas are adequately lit—falling downstairs is a bigger killer than many diseases—you can play tricks with the light. I have star lights, bought in Florence, which throw out rays at random, or so it seems. I have seen corridors lit with candles hung in pairs and a grand hall decked out with a single gigantic chandelier, which also glints and gleams as it moves. The modern style is to use concealed lights, either built flush into the ceilings as they slope upward or buried into the risers

of the stairs so they wash the walls with soft light. Otherwise, shelves of objects can be shown off with hidden lights that also illumine the stairs and floors, or bookshelves can be given lamps with elbows that can be moved between stacks.

Another new feature in these areas is the imaginative use of color. While it is generally a sensible idea to make sure the whole—entrance hall, stairs, landings, and corridors—are treated as one, that does not mean that they have to be boring old white throughout (though that is not necessarily a bad idea).

The color of the stairs—French gray, say—can be contrasted with blocks of brilliant lime or scarlet on a single, visible landing wall or on vistas down corridors, which can be made exciting with plummy shades of eggplant or toast. Color can be used to heighten the underside of the stairs or to bring forward the walls of halls that are oversized. Furniture can be used to the same effect. For example, an overscaled cupboard or armoire under the stairs makes the space seem friendlier, while stuffed easy chairs on landings and cushions in window niches just ask you to stop and lounge for a while, looking out over the stairway window, which may well have the best view in the house.

These areas can also take the strain away from the principal rooms in the house to act as a library, a children's play space, or a small office with desk, chair, and reference library; alternatively, they can be stacked with cupboards and shelves for storing anything from magazines, archives, sheets, and towels to an extra closet or ironing area. I have converted a generous cupboard under the stairs into a galley kitchen with a microwave for guests to use—they love it.

STAIRCASES AND BANISTERS

STAIRS ARE IN THE ARCHITECTURAL NEWS—STEEL, GLASS, CONCRETE, EXOTIC WOODS ARE ALL USED TO MAKE THE BACKBONE OF THE HOUSE INTO SOMETHING MEMORABLE. FROM BEING CINDERELLAS, STAIRCASES ARE NOW THE PRINCESSES OF THE MODERN HOME.

If you have ever doubted the ability of designers to come up with the new, the startling, the imposing, or the just plain wacky, then a look at what can be done with stairs and banisters would convince you what they were capable of.

For, on the face of it, the stairs of a house are the most pedestrian area of all. Their purpose is to get humans, furniture, dogs, cats, and all everyday objects up heights of 50 ft (16 m) or more with the least physical effort possible. For some reason, this area has challenged designers from medieval times to the present more than most other areas—and it is

quite often the staircase, more than any other feature, that attests to a house's age or pretensions. As soon as the fixed staircase with treads and covered risers took the place of mobile ladders, designers started tinkering with it. Indeed, not many centuries after the initial breakthrough was made, architects began to experiment with cantilevered stairs that dispensed with support at one side, with the whole load borne by the stair treads levered far into the single supporting wall.

In the 20th century, the riser often vanished entirely to be replaced with a ladderlike gap, and cantilevered stairs were ever more airy and, ironically, just like the original ladders (and terrifying to people, like me, who suffer from vertigo).

Architects in the last hundred years have also experimented with new materials and technology. One of these materials is glass, with modernists such as Eva Jiricna creating beautiful works of staircase art from layers of glass, both transparent and

LEFT This sculptural staircase consists entirely of a series of wooden cantilevered stairs with helpful risers. There are no handrails, but metal stringing is both elegant and practical.

ABOVE Stairs inserted into a narrow corridor are easily climbed. Since these have a handrail, the designer has done away with the risers, giving a sense of space and a view beyond.

BELOW A series of sensual curves of shuttered concrete disguise the top of the stairs while creating a sense of modernity, light, and space. The owners have decided to leave this area free of decoration.

OPPOSITE, LEFT Clearly inspired by industrial stairs, this set has heavy metal treads without risers, but the elegant banisters of light silvery steel strung through heavier rods show that it has been carefully thought through.

OPPOSITE, RIGHT Some designers do away entirely with any form of banister or support at one edge of the stairs. This gives an elegant ziggurat effect but can be disturbing for people of a nervous disposition, like me.

opaque (which was equally distressing to vertigo sufferers). Glass technology, however, meant that it was now extremely tough and versatile, and not particularly slippery.

Similarly, metals were used in the 20th century for stairs. Metal styles covered the spectrum from the conscious warehouse chic of plates of iron—which were formerly more likely to have appeared on factory floors—to stainless steel and black-painted iron. In total contrast, and reaction, boxed-in cottage stairways with rough walls of interesting stone or early local bricks have been restored where they would once have been ripped out, or even recreated in some new homes.

Designers, too, have become increasingly conscious of ergonomics, and all sorts of theories about the comparative heights of staircase riser and tread have been advanced.

The ideal staircase is the one that needs the least effort to mount. It should have a tread deep enough for a large adult foot, but not one that needs an extra step to cover. It should have a riser which is neither too shallow (so you go up two at once) nor too steep, and an overall width and profile that allows large pieces of furniture to go up and down with minimum discomfort.

Few staircases that I have come across are wide enough to allow a grand piano to be transported from floor to floor—and, perhaps, it is extreme to demand that stairs should be built to accommodate such a rare event when, in modern houses, space is at such a premium. However, queen and kingsize beds have to make the same awkward journey, as do armoires or bookcases. In the early 21st century we are moving home with increasing frequency, so it is important to take such practical considerations into account.

METAL STYLES RANGED FROM THE CONSCIOUS WAREHOUSE CHIC OF IRON PLATES THAT SEEMED TO HAVE COME FROM FACTORY FLOORS TO STAINLESS STEEL AND BLACK-PAINTED IRON.

OPPOSITE, ABOVE AND BELOW
Two views of a very elegant staircase
demonstrate how modernity can be
successfully combined with ruralism.
The unadorned and slightly distressed
wall bricks seem countrified, while
the flexible and riserless staircase is
held together by a central rod, which
supports the treads.

BELOW LEFT Metal makes good rails
and banisters because, unlike wood,
it can be very thin and strong. Curved
steel is here contrasted with a grid of
thinner metal for a Modernist flourish.

RIGHT Stairway areas can be treated
more brutally by designers than would
be possible with living rooms. Here
an unadorned wall of hefty stones has
been accentuated by a single rod of a
handrail that highlights the roughness
of the blocks.

BELOW RIGHT Twentieth-century
factory design is a constant theme
for staircases. What was originally a
practical solution for heavy industry
has now become a statement for
Modernism. The stair rungs here are
pierced to reduce the metal's weight.

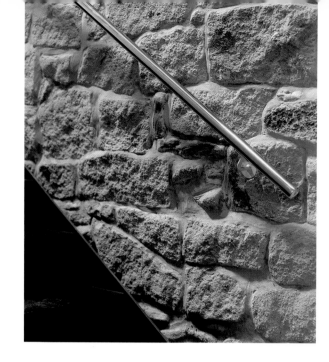

111

It is equally well worth considering the ceilings and angles of your staircase before buying or building a house. My first cottage combined an angle and a sloping ceiling that did not leave room for even an ordinary chest of drawers to be carried up the stairs. The house had been constructed in the 1600s, and, I suppose, at that time no such pieces of furniture existed in the yeoman's home. Our only recourse, as it would be for anyone else who found themselves in the same situation, was to bring everything up through the windows—assuming, that is, that they are big enough.

To the Victorians, spiral stairs were simply a means of changing floors while using up the minimum of space. This style of staircase proliferated during the Victorian era largely because the industrialists of that time were the first to come up with a way of casting iron both cheaply and in large enough sections to make such stairs both economic and possible. Before that, where staircases were too generous for a granary, barn, or workshop, plain ladders were the only alternative. The fact that 19th-century cast-iron stairs are also ornate and stylish is purely a reflection of the fact that British Victorians were incapable of making any object without decorating it.

At some point in the 20th century, spiral stairs made the jump from the factory (I remember a series of spirals from each floor in my first work place, a Victorian newspaper printing works) to the home. Apart from taking up the minimum amount of space—a simple column about 4 ft (slightly more than 1 m) wide—and allowing light to be seen through their treads, so they can be installed in a living room or kitchen, spiral stairs have few advantages. Indeed, they are pretty impractical. It is difficult to carry large objects up and down them (though, to be fair, the lack of walls makes it possible), and they are not comfortable to use.

In spite of the shortcomings of spiral staircases, contemporary designers have continued to enjoy experimenting with them. Their shapes are very seductive, and except in medieval castles, they have rarely been used in domestic settings until now. Heavy black Victorian cast iron has been replaced with all kinds of examples that blend in with the style of the house. Spiral staircases in modern and

OPPOSITE, LEFT **In Mediterranean countries it is very rare for stairs to be made of wood. This combination of whitewashed wall, solid painted handrail, and stair risers made of the ubiquitous terracotta square tiles is the usual solution. And a very good solution it is: practical, cheap, decorative, and simple.**

CENTER, ABOVE **With the arrival of metal banisters in the 18th century, all kinds of flourishes that had been unworkable in wood became possible. The culmination of this trend was seen in the 19th century—as here, where the banisters are the most important part of the stairs.**

CENTER, BELOW **On staircases where metal was not used, wooden banisters became thinner, more elegant, and carefully turned. Most were intended to be painted—almost invariably white—while the rail, made of a more exotic wood, was left as plain, waxed wood.**

ABOVE **Interior designers have always appreciated the possibilities of decorative newel posts. This one harks back to the hefty wooden versions of the 17th century.**

113

ABOVE AND ABOVE RIGHT
This complex staircase has
clearly been influenced by
the intricate wooden detailing
typical of the Arts and Crafts
movement. With decorative
wooden inserts and dowels,
and banisters reduced to a
minimum, it is a fine example
of staircase as showstopper.

RIGHT These stairs are a
product of the same influence
as the staircase above—but
have been designed in a rather
less showy manner. The gaps
between the vertical boards
on one side are accented by
upright paneling on the other.

OPPOSITE, LEFT This staircase
has taken ruralism to its logical
conclusion by using branches
complete with spiky twigs and
bark as its banisters. The rail is
a tree trunk, virtually untreated.
Although esthetically appealing,
it looks uncomfortable to use.

OPPOSITE, RIGHT The rustic
stairs—shown here in context—
mimic the double staircase
of an 18th-century classical
building, indicating that they
are an important part of the
house. Leaving the rest of the
hallway and roof unadorned
gives the decorative effect of
the staircase extra impact.

114

minimalist houses can have fine metal treads cantilevered from the thinnest possible metal central pole and guarded with fine steel banisters—banisters that are essential both for safety and to emphasize the elegant curve of the whole—while new log cabins can go native with wooden stairs bolted onto the equivalent of a single large tree trunk.

There are even clever versions of spirals that have solid guards rather than open banisters, or covered risers rather than open spaces, where the cantilever effect is removed. These have the benefit of being much more secure to walk up.

When does a spiral stop being a spiral? Certainly, a cantilevered 18th-century staircase that curves elegantly upward could not be described as a spiral—a spiral should curve sharply and neatly within its own circle. And when a spiral

is attached to a proper wall, it becomes, simply, a curved staircase. No staircase that is easy to use and lavish of space deserves to be classed with these clever but demanding circular ladders.

Stairway banisters are another giveaway as to a house's date because—while stairs were only one of many areas where designers could play with shape and structure—they are harder to alter than, say, a door, a fireplace, or a bathroom, or virtually any other area of the house. Even roofs get changed because they need regular repair, which staircases, with luck, do not. I did have one relative who took out the stairs in his first house because they were so inconvenient and ugly—only to find he had to use a ladder until a replacement staircase was made. Predictable, perhaps, but true.

THIS PAGE In this example of sophisticated ruralism, the wooden banisters are beautifully proportioned and softly vase-shaped. They and the rail are painted flat white, as is the slightly rough wood floor whose planks lead the eye along an all-white hall to a welcoming source of light.

OPPOSITE, LEFT White-painted staircases rarely disappoint. Here, an intrinsically heavy and stolid set of banisters, handrail, and newel post have been reduced in volume by a coating of white paint, whose effect is to make them vanish against similar-colored walls.

OPPOSITE, ABOVE RIGHT When adventurous house owners wanted grandly carved banisters—but could not afford the lumber—they compromised by making the banisters appear carved and turned. In reality, these curvy blue versions are as flat as planks.

OPPOSITE, BELOW RIGHT Like the banisters shown in the left-hand picture, this set lacks elegance because all its proportions are too heavy. The solution here has been to leave all the wood unpainted—which, as in the all-white scheme, allows the banisters to blend in effortlessly with the hall.

EXOTIC HARDWOODS CHANGED THE BANISTER FROM A HEFTY STATEMENT OF PRESTIGE TO AN ELEGANT STATEMENT OF STYLE.

Virtually all houses are built with their own staircases in position because staircases cannot generally be added later—so there they will remain until they become either rotten or inconvenient.

After the medieval period, when European castles had stairs built within the thickness of the walls, which twisted and turned to discourage invaders, staircases became both wide and shallow. It is obvious why this was the case in the great palaces of Europe, where stone staircases had handrails built into their walls, but even in small manors and farmhouses the steps of oak and elm were wide, shallow, and easily mounted. In all of them, it is possible to imagine descending in a full hooped skirt or crinoline. Banisters to these stairs were just as generous. Usually, they were of solid and massive oak with chunky turned finials and handrails smoothly carved from large branches.

Where solid wood was too expensive, people devised faux banisters that looked as though they were solid spirals, but which were, in fact, theatrical cutouts. These flat banisters have recently been revived in such materials as plywood and composite board and painted in heritage colors.

It was the arrival of exotic hardwoods from both the East and West Indies that transformed the banister from a hefty statement of prestige to an elegant statement of style. Oak and walnut were not suitable

117

for making such slender posts and rails, but the iron strength of mahogany and teak was. In both mahogany and teak banisters, the stair rail was rounded off with twirls and flourishes when it reached its most important point on the ground floor.

Jacobean and Georgian banister styles both mixed and mingled different styles of turned support in a single staircase along with detailing at the edge of the tread. By the 19th century, the mahogany had become even heftier, but in the place of thinly turned wood, ornate cast iron made an appearance. This was in much the same style as the charming verandas of the French Quarter of New Orleans and the high Regency town of Brighton.

Although this ironwork can be recreated today by using new castings or balusters found in architectural salvage yards, the mahogany handrail can only rarely be found. One alternative is to use soft wood carved to match, but painted white.

Modern banisters have become ever more reduced so they are frequently little more than wires strung on slightly denser poles. They are made of painted iron, like the Victorian ones but without any ornament, or from the 20th-century metals, chrome, or stainless steel.

The ability to use slender materials for the balusters and handrails has also made it possible to claw back some extra space for the stairs themselves. As a consequence, stairs in ordinary homes are probably wider today than they have been at any point since the 17th century.

OPPOSITE, ABOVE LEFT AND CENTER Metal spiral staircases evolved in the 19th century as a way of moving between floors with the minimum of wasted space. This modern version emphasizes the spinal effect of such a spiral by accenting the heavy metal central rod and the propellor-shaped treads. The rails of silvery metal follow the curve with glints of light.

OPPOSITE, BELOW LEFT This is the conventional spiral staircase as used in factories and offices. It has a chunkier line than the one above, with the rod made up of "vertebrae."

BELOW LEFT This open-air staircase, not quite attached to the rough log outside walls, is clearly influenced by factory spirals, but has enclosed walls rather than open banisters.

BELOW Double curved metal rods support this open set of stairs, which are dark against a light wall for maximum decorative value. A light source from above also adds shifting, curved shadows.

Another revival not seen since the 17th century is that of the gallery—which is distinct from a landing in that it has open rails rather than closed walls. The intention of the gallery is to allow light into landing areas while uniting these spaces with the stairs and floors below.

Ideally, galleries should be used as rooms. I have seen gallery kitchens and bedrooms in open-plan houses (and I've also seen gallery bathrooms but, since they are hardly private, I don't recommend them). These large and light corridors make good libraries, music rooms and offices. In large houses, they can also be used for storage (perhaps removing the need to carry everything from a basement washing machine to an airing cupboard at the top of the house) or for practical purposes such as wardrobes, which don't have to be in bedrooms, ironing

areas or computer and television spaces. It is essential to keep them tidy. Unlike rooms, halls and stairways are always on view.

Galleries are also excellent places for showing off. A gallery is the ideal spot to house a collection of fossils, groups of favourite pictures or large quilts draped on the sizeable walls. The word gallery originally described a narrow space for walking either in a house or around a covered area between house and garden. It was only later that it came to mean a place where pictures and objects were displayed.

Lighting, flooring and furnishings should be deployed skilfully in galleries. If objects are displayed on shelves or behind glass, lighting can be hidden, giving the area a pleasant glow. Display cases should be in sympathy with the design of the house and the floor used to add length or width to the whole.

A GALLERY IS THE IDEAL SPOT TO DISPLAY A GROUP OF FOSSILS, FAVORITE PICTURES, OR LARGE QUILTS.

OPPOSITE, LEFT AND RIGHT
Although the overall appearance of
this set of stairs and overhead gallery
is of rough lumber simply nailed
together, its actual construction was
a far more complex process. Straight
and heavy tree trunks have been
carefully rounded and smoothed, but—
since the ends have been left jutting
forward—the whole structure remains
visible. Wisely, the owners have not
even attempted to decorate this
massive area. A single plain chandelier
hangs from the ceiling, and a tribal rug
is casually slung over the handrail.

RIGHT This cool stair and gallery
scheme could have come straight
from a luxury liner. The combination
of metal pillars, good-quality wood,
and the slightly industrial feeling recall
the feel of a grand ship. The gallery
and bar beneath manage to double
the available space.

BELOW This is the same area
seen from a higher level. The feeling
throughout the apartment is of squares
and rectangles, emphasized by the
stark black and white decor and the
strong railings of the gallery. Even the
abstract painting contributes to this.

LEFT Stairways are often dark, even poky. The trick is to use color to reduce the sense of enclosure. This set is monochrome, with even the floor painted as light a shade as possible. Light and shadow are used to emphasize angles and features.

BELOW LEFT This stairway, set between two narrow walls and without any natural light, has been deliberately darkened by using a deeper shade of paint than necessary. What makes it distinct is the white on the baseboards and stair risers, which gives the whole thing a sculptural quality.

CENTER AND OPPOSITE, ABOVE RIGHT The owners have played fast and loose with what was originally a classical corridor. Colors of walls and doors have been reversed (doors are usually lighter), while the paterae and the ceiling are picked out in scarlet.

OPPOSITE, BELOW RIGHT If you own a staircase as lovely as this 18th-century one, don't mess it up. Plain colors accentuate the generous width of the stairs and the subtly ornate banister, while the hanging lamp and carefully placed longcase clock are classical in their simplicity.

COLOR

CHOOSING COLORS FOR NARROW SPACES IS QUITE A CHALLENGE. THE BIG PROBLEM IS THAT COLORS DO NOT HAVE A CHANCE TO DIFFUSE BETWEEN WALLS. ANY STRONG COLOR YOU PICK WILL BECOME CONCENTRATED AND MORE POWERFUL. THAT IS NOT ALWAYS A BAD THING—BUT IT IS IMPORTANT TO BE AWARE OF IT.

As someone who once—misguidedly—painted an entire five-story staircase scarlet, I can faithfully say that picking colors for narrow spaces is not easy. And most landings and staircases are either narrow or very narrow. In my case, the whole sixty-two steps' worth thrummed with mindbending color like a disco lightshow. Red shot back and forth from wall to wall, concentrating the brilliance as it went. The flat-white banisters and stair edges turned shrimp pink—and it looked just awful.

As a result of the scarlet disaster, I like my general spaces to be neutral. The original idea for red came from a wonderful 18th-century staircase in a grand Dublin townhouse that looked quite superb allied with a diagonally laid limestone floor. If you are lucky enough to have something similar, then do try such a scarlet or, for that matter, malachite green, sapphire blue, or lime yellow. Team it with white so that the elegant lines are sharply angled and emphasized. The rest of us—with poky, boxed-in areas of dreary wood or plain, practical stairs that do nothing but get people from here to there—will have to dream on. Yes, scarlet would be wonderful, but better to settle for a neutral shade.

I don't for a moment want to spoil your fun—even with a neutral shade, you can still get pretty sassy. For instance, while the walls should stay plain, woodwork looks good either lighter or darker. Darker colors add solidity, a rustic feeling, or a swerve to Victorian values. They are good in large 19th-century areas, especially when the quality of the woodwork is high. Heavy paneled doors, carefully profiled baseboards and sculptural banisters

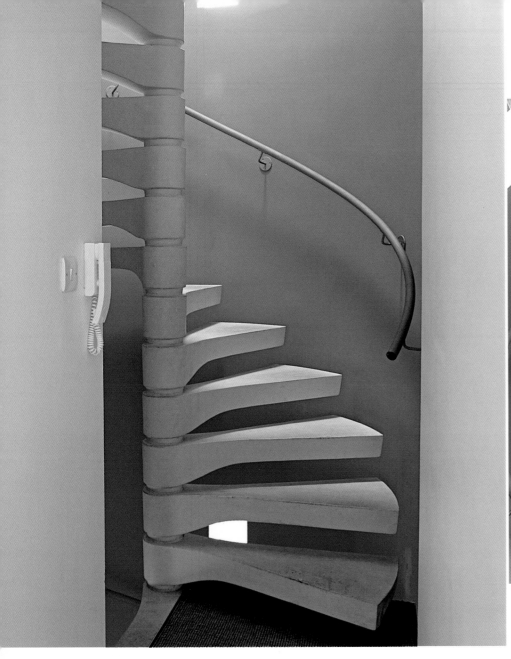

ABOVE AND ABOVE RIGHT
Converting old industrial buildings into homes provides plenty of opportunity for architectural swagger and flourish. These stairs have been installed in a former leather works in London, and are at the cutting edge of contemporary design. Every unnecessary detail has been removed, allowing the stark, precast polished concrete to stand out, like vertebrae, against grey-blue walls. The railing has been finished in matt grey, with industrial lighting fastened to the walls at regular intervals.

OPPOSITE, ABOVE LEFT An ornate Italian iron chair has been carefully positioned against a background of soft blues and whites to attract the eye to the end of a corridor.

all do well in somber shades. Imagine that they are made of solid mahogany, and you will get some idea of the effect.

Lighter shades are preferable for dark and narrow areas that need all the help they can get. A staircase or hall painted entirely white may be too minimal and clinical, but by varying the colors a tone, you can emphasize the woodwork against the plain white walls. Everything can be pale—the underside of the staircase (which adds hugely to the airiness of a hall), the banisters, the entire area of stairs and landings. You don't even need a carpet if you paint the stair treads—though you'll certainly need to be a dab hand with a mop.

Fashions in colors come and go, and the craze of the moment is for neutrals in shades of off-white mixed with black, gray, or earth shades.

Magnolia and cream are currently in the ashcan of taste—from which, no doubt, they will emerge in time refreshed. But consider all those undemanding shades of bone, string, canvas, stone, dead salmon, and mouse that are offered today in the heritage paint selections. These were the colors used for the narrow corridors below stairs in the great European houses, and as you will see if you visit kitchen corridors and servants' quarters, they look good together.

Similar shades and tones have been used in old working homes, farmhouses, and cottages, up the back stairs and along the winding corridors. These were areas where the intention was to be practical—showing off was kept for the parlor and dining room. And, since this is what we've been conditioned to expect, it is constantly restful.

IN DARK AND NARROW AREAS.
EVERYTHING CAN BE PALE: THE
UNDERSIDE OF THE STAIRCASE,
THE BANISTERS, THE ENTIRE
AREA OF STAIRS AND LANDINGS.

ABOVE AND LEFT Clearly the work of an experienced interior designer, this stairway was inspired by the collection of 19th-century blue-and-white Staffordshire plates displayed on the flanking wall. The bold check wallpaper—whose blue is picked up in the plain walls and the color edging the stair treads—are all reflected in the colors of the china.

The background for stairs and corridors needs a certain blandness because you can work on it like an unassertive canvas. In the very first house we owned—a pleasant Yorkshire cottage with an eccentric double staircase (the bathroom had stairs of its own)—we painted all the tongue-and-groove doors with blue and white stripes.

Our next home, a Jacobean clothmaker's house built of millstone grit, which brooded in its own West Yorkshire valley, had wildly generous stairs and landings with late 18th-century doors marching its length in pairs. We painted it greenish lemon (I have an aversion to egg yellow) and picked out the elegant panels of the doors in three shades of gray. In both houses—indeed, in every house we've ever lived in—the stairs doubled as a gallery for the paintings and prints that we kept on buying.

Paneled doors like this, particularly prevalent in middle-range 18th- and 19th-century British houses, lend themselves to clever coloring. The main frame can be a single shade and the inner panels either a variation of this or a contrast, while the edge of the panel is yet a third color. My gray doors had darker frames and lighter panels with a middle tone for the panels' edges; but now I think I might try either black or white or—I still hanker after it—a thin sliver of brilliant lacquer red. At the same time, the baseboards that run between the doors could echo the scheme with the same three colors. And, as you will see here, it's even possible to color the stairs the same way.

When you are thinking about flossing up the doors, remember that what you do can be seen from inside the room into which they lead as well as in the stairs or halls. It doesn't matter if the door's two sides differ, but they shouldn't shout at each other.

Another trick with paneled doors is to wallpaper the inner panels. Toile de Jouy is especially effective—you can allude to, though not copy, the pattern in the curtains—as do pictorial wallpapers or those with a generous repeat. If you

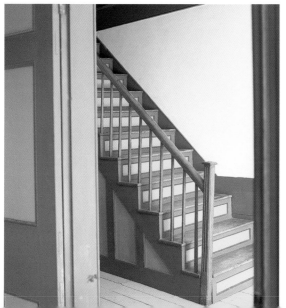

OPPOSITE, LEFT Halls and stairways are areas where it is possible to be rather more decoratively adventurous than elsewhere in the house. In this case a strong combination of colors of equal weight has been used. But, since both are natural earth tones, the impression is elegant and rich.

OPPOSITE, RIGHT In the 18th and 19th centuries, it was extremely common to use fancy paint techniques along the corridors and up the stairs. Here, soft ocher marbling gives a friendly informality to a severe area.

ABOVE Invigorating is the message conveyed by this clever combination of colors in a hall. While the walls have been left soft white, three contrasting primaries have been used to decorate the doors: moody blue for the main parts, ocher for the door panels, and scarlet on the panel moldings.

LEFT A more general view of the hall above shows that the same three shades—soft blue, ocher, and scarlet— have also been painted on the stair risers to give the impression that they, like the doors, are paneled.

LEFT It takes courage to ignore completely the very fine decorative features of this French apartment, yet the lines of the paneling have not been taken into account in a scheme that uses a combination of grays in wide, vertical stripes.

BELOW LEFT If your landings are dark, there is no need to fight it— go along with what you have. This corridor has been painted black, with blackboard paint and a chalked sketch to attract the eye at the end. The "jack" light doubles as sculpture.

can find a paper where the pattern, when cut, neatly fits the panel, experiment with it. It can look amazingly impressive.

Although I am generally against wallpaper on stairs—any pattern is extremely difficult to hang on complex walls—it can be used in the halls between the flights. Paper, well chosen, can make a ground-floor entrance hall extremely welcoming and also help to divide it from the stairs beyond. But there should be a connection between the two—a major color in the paper could match the plain walls of the stairs, or the pattern could be copied on curtains higher up. Another trick is to upholster chairs or window seats on upper-floor landings to match the paper on the hall below, which is, in turn, curtained in the same color as the plain walls.

The higher the house—and, of course, the stairs—the more important it is to have continuity. It's not a good idea to start the ascent with gray

walls, then suddenly burst into soft pink or mushroom. Instead, the landings can vary the color, turning, say, from soft gray to stronger blue or from white to stone, with the staircase beyond continuing in your designated stair color. But it will only work if there is a clear cut-off point between the two. Similarly, you can make color changes if the stairs themselves change. In many 18th- and 19th-century houses, at both basement and top-floor levels the stairs suddenly become less grand and painted wood takes the place of a mahogany handrail. You can change the color pace here, too.

Perhaps hardest of all are stairs that are totally boxed in, hidden in the width of a wall and meant to be kept out of sight. These are often the back stairs leading to secondary rooms and, therefore, not felt to be worth spending money on. Or they could be in tiny farm cottages, old-fashioned row houses, or houses converted from industrial or

OPPOSITE, RIGHT Pure color can work its own miracles with the addition of light and shade. This beauifully curved staircase is accentuated by strong light, which throws a deep and curving shadow on the opposite wall.

THIS PAGE A multiplicity of natural light sources have been harnessed to introduce interest to this long corridor. White, textured, translucent, matt, lacy, and shiny all contribute to the cool sensuality of the area.

COLORING STAIRS
AND HALLS NEEDS
BRAVERY: NOTHING
WILL BE ACHIEVED
BY TONING DOWN
A BRIGHT IDEA.

agricultural buildings. Bleakest of all are those echoing stone, concrete, or metal stairs and landings in tenements and redundant factories.

Don't even try to make them cozy with flower prints or deep carpets—it will just seem incongruous. But try to think like an art gallery: clothe the clanging stairs in a plain gray carpet or sisal matting, and paint the walls steely blue or plaster pink. If you are brave, go for the distressed-ruin look or the minimalist exaggeration of warehouse chic. I, personally, wouldn't color these clanking spaces in any dark shades, but with dramatic lighting, even gloss black and steel can acquire glamour.

Bravery in coloring stairs and halls is often its own reward. Nothing was ever achieved by toning down a bright idea because it was too adventurous. If it turns out you were just plain wrong, do what I did with my scarlet walls. The paint had hardly had time to dry before I admitted my mistake—and turned them soft gray.

RIGHT The basic dullness of this entrance hall and stolid staircase with its unfashionable dog leg has been retrieved by the sugared-almond treatment of the walls. Pink, sky blue, and apricot are combined with simple wooden doors and stairs.

FAR RIGHT ABOVE Since this landing and corridor are so stylish, even pink looks cool. Note how the color changes blend in different areas and how the lighting of the dark wall creates "arches" at the top.

FAR RIGHT BELOW This entire corridor has been kept a single, soft yellow. which has the effect of emphasizing the pretty barrel vaulting of the ceiling with its arched light toward the rear. The nicely paneled doors have, in each case, been stripped back to bleached wood.

BELOW A staircase, at its simplest, is a mere succession of treads with some means of support. This set could not be more basic—double rod supports and heavy plain treads with no form of riser. It is beautiful because of the quality of the wood used for the treads, which has been left utterly simple.

RIGHT Another set of stairs has been reduced to a minimum, but here the designer has at least added risers. The combination of exotic wood, unadorned, and a flying steel newel makes these stairs a sculpture.

INSET A simple series of stairs is varied by short, well-lit landings.

FAR RIGHT The dark and shiny wooden floor transforms the strong scheme of this spacious entrance hall and stairs into something quite memorable. The owners have exploited the hall's architectural qualities to the maximum by adding impressive pieces of furniture, strategically placed.

FLOORING

FLOORING IN THE AREAS OF STAIRWAYS, HALLS, AND LANDINGS NEEDS TO BE PRACTICAL AND HARDWEARING, TO SHRUG OFF DIRT BROUGHT IN FROM OUTSIDE, AND TO BE SAFE. BUT THESE AREAS ALSO OFFER A CHANCE TO MAKE A STATEMENT ABOUT THE WHOLE HOUSE. THEY SHOULD BE WARM, WELCOMING, AND IN KEEPING WITH WHAT IS BEHIND THE CLOSED DOORS LEADING OFF THEM.

While in most respects halls and landings are the poor relations in a house, their floors, curiously, are given top treatment. I remember one—rude—Italian visitor to our London house describing it as a *casuccio* (hovel) because the staircase was made of wood. This was a far cry from floors made of immaculately laid terra-cotta tiles.

It was this classical insistence on good solid entrance floors and stairs—a Roman floor discovered untouched in Pompeii had the famous mosaic of a dog over the words *cave canem*—that was translated everywhere in the West into a whole series of flagged entrance halls. These vary from the beautiful apricot flagstones of England's Cotswold Hills, of such fine texture that they develop a luster as they age, to the hefty York flagsones of gray sandstone; and to the limestones of French chateaux and the multicolored, Moorish-influenced tiles of Iberia.

Such floors were laid from medieval times on, and where there was no indigenous stone, square clay tiles, bricks, or quarry tiles, the equivalent of Italian cotta tiles, were laid instead. Where there was plenty of wood in different textures and colors—ash, beech, oak, and elm—intricate patterns of parquet floors emerged, each one designed and laid for the specific area. In

133

LEFT Stairways and halls often have the best floors in the house—and the trick is to appreciate them. The lovely parquet floor of this London home is given depth and tone by a soft waxing, and the rougher texture of the rugs is used to emphasize its quality.

ABOVE Once again, high-quality parquet has been given prominence—on this occasion, it has been contrasted with a completely different texture. The carefully laid coconut door mat (they can be made to order) separates the doorway from the hall.

the grander houses, especially Palladian stately homes, entrance halls were copied from Greek and Italian models and made with imported white squares of marble, set diagonally and interspersed with neat, smaller black stone squares. It was easy for Andrea Palladio—the marble area of Carrara was just up the road—but elsewhere marble had to be imported or hard-wearing granites and fossil-bearing faux marbles used instead.

These floors are almost always left unadorned apart from an occasional polish—not even a large Oriental rug is needed—and they cover the entire hall area leading toward a sweep of grand stone stairs, usually in unassertive pale gray stone.

If you are lucky enough to have a house with its original (or later) stone floor, give thanks. You won't need to carpet it at all,

and cleaning will involve only the occasional sweep of a mop. Furthermore, it will last hundreds of years with only slight wearing in the busiest areas. The hollows and dips caused by the tread of innumerable feet over the decades should be welcomed for they say, clearer than anything, that your house is centuries old.

Halls and stairways have always also been the most used—and therefore most worn—parts of the house, and it is for this reason that money is spent in laying them with durable materials. In Victorian times, stone gave way to encaustic tiles, which are both colorful and stylish, and can be seen in British churches revamped at this period and in 19th-century British townhouses. Again, rejoice—they have passed their unfashionable moment and are considered a

LEFT This is a rougher parquet floor than the one shown on the opposite page. Its wood is lower quality and the blocks are larger, but it has the real advantage of two contrasting strips of darker lumber. These delineate the shape of the hallway area.

ABOVE If you don't have integral features in your wooden hallway floor, you can create them. Here, the plain everyday planks of a softwood floor have been painted to look a great deal grander.

RIGHT The charm of this up-to-date stairway lies in the bleached stair treads, whose lovely pale gray allows the grain and knots to be visible. The soft blue of the walls contrasts well, as do the monochrome pictures.

plus by everyone. Where encaustic was considered too loud or too expensive, quarry tiles were laid. These are generally arranged in patterns of alternating black and red—simple diagonals and squares for inner halls and corridors, and more complex designs at the entrance.

While, today, encaustic tiles can only be found in salvage yards, it is quite possible to buy new quarry tiles (though salvaged ones look more authentic). A builder who once laid some new quarry tiles for me went to the trouble of breaking a few to give them that old, distressed look.

As a substitute for tiles, you can lay concrete, scratch it into tilelike patterns, and paint it black and red. Flagstones are also available from salvage firms, and one good wheeze is to buy thinner stone roof slates and cement them in. Since

UNLIKE ORDINARY ROOMS, STAIRWAYS AND HALLS ARE CONSTANTLY SEEN FROM DIFFERENT HEIGHTS AND PERSPECTIVES— DEPENDING ON THE ANGLE FROM WHICH YOU APPROACH THEM.

flagstones are generally sold by weight, this works out much cheaper and, as long as the stones are well laid, they will not break. New flagstones are also easily found, but they are not cheap. Most are of French limestone, which is a lovely light creamy color and adds light to any space.

Indeed, unless your halls and stairways are already brilliantly lit, it is advisable to floor them in a pale material. This can be pale stone or concrete with a color additive, soft textured seagrass or sisal, which is both hard-wearing and adaptable, or simply layers of paint or whitewash over the wood. Good solid paint such as that brushed onto yachts is a hard-wearing option, while pickling wood lets the color sink into the grain. Ordinary flat oil paint also works well, especially if you give it a slight polish—though not so much that it becomes slippery and dangerous. In all these cases, maintenance involves simply a good mopping once in a while. Don't worry if certain areas get worn or chipped—it all adds to the impression of shabby chic.

I wouldn't, however, recommend a pale carpet for either hall or stairs. They get dirty very quickly, and even cleaning won't bring out some stains. So, real carpet is only an option if you don't want to add to the light. You may not need to if the walls and ceilings are pale, and if this is the case, I would choose something like dark charcoal worsted. Most worsteds in natural wools are

OPPOSITE These three pictures show the same set of stairs at different levels. From below, the lack of risers and the supporting beam below the treads are the main areas of interest, but this impression totally vanishes when you descend, seeing the stairs from above. The treads seem nearly bland, and the darker banister is the main interest.

THIS PAGE A trick is used in this staircase and landing to draw the whole area together: the level part of the floor has been divided into chunks whose width and depth are similar to those of each stair tread. A banister rail divides the two like an abstract painting. The Chinese chair adds the only decoration to a formal and serious room.

OPPOSITE AND LEFT White stone floors such as this one, with its inset of black marble, have been made to this pattern since Roman times. Not only is it graceful and more complex than straight squares, but also the insets add strength to the structure. The monochromes of the floor have given the owners the opportunity to play with plenty of colors and textures, from squares of stained and molded glass inset into wide frames to strongly painted furniture and fixtures.

BELOW LEFT A new invention made encaustic tiles like these a possibility in the 19th century. The complex colors and patterns were highly fashionable, even in churches. Then they fell out of favor and were ripped away. If you have some, flaunt them.

BELOW The gentle curve of the stairs and the simplicity of their construction make possible a very busy, colorful floor. This pattern derives from Moorish tiles and, while complex, is controlled in color.

hardwearing and adapt easily to all the angles of a staircase. Their lack of pile also seems to reduce the dirt. Don't be tempted to carpet your stairs or halls in a shade that is already dirt-colored–those dull muds and coffees always look pedestrian.

These areas can benefit from changes of pace, color, and texture, though I wouldn't change all three at once. If you start off with a gray flagstoned floor, you could paint your wooden staircase white and give it a rustic covering in gray just a shade different. If this covering has a herringbone or diaper weave, so much the better. If, on the other hand, your main entrance hall is neutral–white walls, bland wood floor leading to a modern staircase with steel banisters–then you can startle the eye with a brilliant runner up the stairs. It can be plain scarlet or navy or a multicolored, striped runner, traditional on stairs perhaps because its stripes lead the eye up.

If the hall is multipatterned–those encaustic tiles, swirling linoleum, or an Oriental rug covering the floorboards–then increase the simplicity of the stairs by picking just one or two shades from the floor and repeating them on the stairs. I am not particularly keen on the idea of stair carpets

with ultra-busy patterns (though they are good at hiding dirty marks) because they disguise the lines of the stairs and restrict what can be done with the walls and ceilings.

Similarly, I like the functional corridors and landings that lead from the main hall and stairs to be simply floored. This is mainly because plain carpets or boards are easier to walk on (wild patterns can be deceptive and cause you to trip) and because I like to let the excitement and busyness of these areas come from something more original than a carpet.

The enthusiasms of designers should be kept under severe control when it comes to this area. Left to themselves, they will turn the plain and pragmatic into something much more bombastic. While some aspects of landings and stairways do

need careful and expert attention—lighting, for example—floor treatments should be kept as simple as possible. This is not to say that they can't be beautiful—what is lovelier than wooden boards waxed to a soft glow or ancient tiles showing the wear of centuries?—but once these constricted parts of the house get over-complex, the spaces will be spoiled. Therefore, if you have natural good-looking floors, don't bother to carpet them unless the noise is too much; if you must have a carpet, go for a plain version in a strong-wearing weave or, in smaller houses, those endearing striped runners that have recently come back into fashion.

If you leave the floors (and ceilings) of these busy areas neatly plain, then you can go to town on the walls. But that's another story.

WHAT IS LOVELIER THAN WOODEN BOARDS WAXED TO A SOFT GLOW OR ANCIENT TILES SHOWING THE WEAR OF CENTURIES?

ABOVE LEFT Carpeting your staircase and landings reduces the noise and controls the dust. This severe setting relies on a light neutral carpet to set off the soft blue of the walls.

LEFT Carpets can be as decorative and distinctive as a wooden or stone floor. Given the generous and eccentric curves along this corridor, the owner had the clever idea of echoing them in the pattern of the carpet.

OPPOSITE, ABOVE LEFT AND RIGHT Given a rather narrow set of stairs, especially in the country, a striped drugget is often the answer. It acts like a carpet in reducing noise but, being narrower and vertically striped, it will help to increase the apparent width of each stair. Here the stairs' stripe is subtly varied from that of the hall.

OPPOSITE, BELOW LEFT AND RIGHT Notice how a set of stairs can look completely different, depending on which angle you see it from. This same set appears almost conventional when seen from above. From the side, it is apparent how open it really is, seeming to float from the wooden floor.

ABOVE LEFT Modern technology has transformed methods of lighting, which can be as obtrusive or secret as you could wish. The owners of this upstairs landing have used a combination of low-voltage lights to make a pattern on the ceiling, but combined it with natural light from shade-covered windows and built-in lights just above floor level.

LEFT Diffused light created by translucent shades or other covers placed in front of both daylight and artificial light provides an overall soft glow. This is excellent for halls and landings where close work such as reading is never done, but where you need to see steps and obstacles.

ABOVE Since there is no need for strong light spots in most halls and stairways, you can play around with levels. Here, built-in lights are placed a foot or so above the floor and the same distance from the ceiling.

OPPOSITE Open-plan living allows a multiplicity of lights and light sources. This space makes full use of the options: built-in lights used as a pattern feature, hanging lights for overall brightness, and, in the working area beyond, strong lights that create pools of brilliance. Hidden lights also contribute to the whole—a pair on either side of the cabinet add a couple of hotspots, while overhead lighting gives a general low glow.

LIGHTING

AREAS THAT LINK ROOMS SHOULD BE ACCOMMODATING AT ALL HOURS, AND THE IMPORTANCE OF GETTING THE LIGHTING RIGHT CANNOT BE OVERSTRESSED. HIDDEN LIGHTS IN FLOORS AND CEILINGS WORK WELL EVEN IN OLDER HOUSES, AS DO WALL LIGHTS. PLAN FOR GOOD BACKGROUND LIGHTING WITH SPOTS OF INTEREST.

Those parts of a house not designated as rooms are frequently windowless—or, at best, dark and shadowed. They therefore need to be lit even more carefully than the traditional rooms.

Good lighting in such spaces is not only desirable but important. While you don't need to install the pinpoint lights to read in comfort, use a chopping knife without damaging your fingers, or put on makeup accurately, you do need to be able to see well enough to avoid falling downstairs. Falls on stairs are a major cause of accidents in the home—and

I wouldn't be surprised to learn that most of them are caused by lighting that dazzles or falls in pools, leaving other areas dark, or which encourages shadows when it is crucial to see clearly. Obviously, when lighting these risky areas, safety must take priority over sexy design features. Even the most dogmatic designers don't really deserve to break their necks falling down their own stylish stairs.

But, apart from safety, another important consideration is that these functional areas should convey a sense of airiness and welcome. Quite often, stairwells and landings have no outside windows, or certainly not ones that can be opened. Even if the air is fresh and sweet—circulated by open doors leading leading from ventilated rooms—the impression will be that it is not. If there are windows up the stairs, the sunlight streaming in will give the impression of freshness, and these windows should have the minimum of curtaining possible. But,

THIS PAGE Corridors can be inviting, leading the eye and the feet toward what promise to be interesting treats. From the early 20th century, curves were often incorporated in buildings to create extra drama, as happened in this house dating from 1937. The passage is skillfully lit: nothing is overt, but pools of light focus on distant doors and on the architectural features of niches in the curves.

OPPOSITE, ABOVE AND BELOW One feature typical of modern design is the use of pools of light that have no apparent source. The sophisticated series of halls and stairways in this house is given added interest by the subtle use of sculptural partitions and cubist elements—all lit in such a way that they resemble monumental works of art.

THE SKILL IS TO CREATE AN ATMOSPHERE THAT WORKS BY BOTH DAY AND NIGHT, TAKING ADVANTAGE OF SPACES WHICH, UNLIKE THE MAIN ROOMS, DO NOT REVEAL THEMSELVES ALL AT ONCE.

if there are no openings for natural light, you will have to create the impression of sunrays by trickery instead. One common trick, employed from the 18th century on, is the skylight, which allows maximum daylight to stream down the entire length of the stairwell with the added bonus that it is toplighting. If possible, you could create a small, hidden, glassed area in the roof. Another trick is to put in plain glass doors that lead into rooms off the staircase and borrow the light from their windows. In a new house, small openings with wide reveres can be designed at strategic angles of the stairs—rather like arrow slits in medieval castles—which are surprisingly effective.

These various tricks can be supplemented by introducing artificial light to increase the effect. Light "borrowed" from other rooms can be enhanced by placing table or floor lamps in areas of the room where their rays can mingle with the daylight. If they can be hidden behind doorways, so much the better. Toplighters inside a room near the door will have a similar effect.

The wide ledges created by the obtuse opening angles of the wall slits can also be used for table lights or lights concealed in the opening's top. All the staircase lights can be activated from below with a single switch so that, however tall the stairs, beams of light beckon you up.

New houses are much easier to deal with than old. If you are building from scratch, you can make sure your architect allows maximum light to percolate into the halls and stairway through a variety of tricks. The skylight is easy to incorporate, even on more than one floor; so are entrance areas made up of huge glass windows that flood the hall and subsequent stairs. Other schemes can create semi open-plan rooms so that walls are stripped away wherever possible, thereby incorporating some of the passageways into the well-lit room

itself. Landing windows can equally become walls of glass flooding at least two floors with daylight. You can even put spiral staircases into rooms and do away with staircases altogether, but they may be very inconvenient for moving furniture.

Old houses are more of a problem, especially if they are subject to heritage controls. If planning permission does not allow for new windows, skylights, or glass walls, then I fear you are stuck with artificial light both by day and night. This is not a complete disaster—even the cleverest natural lighting scheme will need help at night.

The question is whether your lighting by day and night will always appear artificial, or whether you will try more trickery to make it seem like daylight. If the latter, you can always create pretend windows and skylights, especially as today you can get lighting systems that approximate the color of daylight

as opposed to the mellow yellow light of electric bulbs. A false skylight can be built at the top of the stairs or on landings, with multiple bulbs giving diffused light behind panels of opaque glass. It can be very effective as long as you remember to remove the dead flies and other giveaways. False windows can be made to give a similar effect by concealing false lighting behind opaque glass or blinds. Putting mirrors on the sides of the window opening will add to the brightness.

Daylight can also be simulated by concealed, bright lighting that appears to come from hidden windows. The light shines strongly through an open door or false window, illuminating the corridor and stairs in front of the door and intimating shafts of brilliant sunlight beyond. It is effective and very welcoming. Then there is the option of artificial

OPPOSITE, LEFT Strong lights are built into the staircase wall at baseboard level, each giving the treads a beam of brightness. This also makes a pattern out of the stairs.

OPPOSITE, RIGHT While the stairs on the left are colored and lit dramatically to cast strong shadows, the colors of this cool scheme bring out small shade differences while making the stair risers and treads perfectly clear.

RIGHT Many staircases have no form of natural light. This can be turned to advantage by creating a lighting scheme that is constant both day and night. These deep niches have been specially created for characterful lamps.

BELOW RIGHT It is becoming common to put lights at ground or near-ground level—the technology means uplighters and side lights are far safer and less easily damaged than before. They cast a good light at floor level and wash the walls with softer light above.

BELOW Stair-level lights can either be unobtrusive or rather more individual. The stair level light in this house appears to come from a metal grill.

lighting that is quite blatant. There are many clever ways of using today's technology to interesting effect in dark areas. In addition to concealed ceiling lights or spotlights washing the walls, concealed lights can be positioned high up on the walls for a general glow, or a foot or so above the level of the baseboard, where they will light up the floor or the angles of the stairs.

Real wall lights can be wired into staircase walls, an effective way of pulling the attention up. They can be anything from the full classical glint of gilt sconces with mirrors and false candles to ultramodern steel versions. One really lovable scheme I've seen used in an ancient house was a series of candles stuck into wall hangings like coathangers, which were lit every evening. Anyone lazier could use electric candles.

The new fiber-optic systems can be as visible and adaptable as you need—dozens of tiny spots can twinkle around ceilings and walls, or a snake of lighting can be hidden above a specially constructed molding, whether at ceiling or floor level, to create an overall glow.

Nor should you forget the simplest system of all—a series of elegant hanging lights that fall from each horizontal ceiling above the landings. This is traditional, and it works. There are plenty of styles to choose from—18th-century crystal or modern, steely chandeliers, Indian hundi lights or Italian star lights, pierced Moroccan lanterns made of tin or Japanese globes made of rice paper.

Heavy iron chandeliers with genuine candles above an ancient stairwell cast marvelous flickering shadows and give off an evocative, waxy smell.

148

OPPOSITE, LEFT One way to make halls friendlier is to add a few table lamps on narrow chests or console tables. If the overall lighting is adequate, table lamps create intimate pools of light, emphasizing objects and pictures.

OPPOSITE, ABOVE RIGHT Hanging lights are a good solution in long, narrow halls. They reduce the apparent height of the ceiling because the eye is caught by the fixture. This corridor also has a wall light placed to create a welcome in the distance.

OPPOSITE, BELOW RIGHT The concept of stealing light from other rooms has been around since classical times. Given a well-lit living room or dining area, an internal window can be made to give the impression of daylight in a hall. This is only possible if you are happy to have the lighted room on constant display. It won't do for bedrooms.

LEFT Another way of borrowing light is to insert skylights in a corridor's ceiling. It works easily if there is sky above the light, which can be augmented with hidden artificial light at night. But even without any daylight, a skylight can be made to appear as though bright sun is flooding in.

ABOVE You don't need to be a design guru to know that bright daylight is the best of all features in any space. If the window faces anything but north, you can add regular sun to that recipe and, quite likely, a view. This sweeping area has all three. Full use has been made of this fact by sliding the corridor into the living room so it gets daylight, too. Another clever feature is the high, curved window in the corridor, which does not demand too much attention. The whole area therefore has been made to appear light and sunny.

IF THEY ARE PROPERLY TREATED, STAIRCASES AND LANDINGS CAN BE MAGICAL PLACES AT NIGHT—FILLED WITH ANGLES, SHADOWS, FLICKERS, AND MYSTERY.

After some experiments in using the house—deciding where you need good lighting, where a suggestion of illumination will be enough, where switches are necessary—you should carefully plan exactly how these areas will be lit. Take the whole lot in one sweep, from entrance hall, up as many flights of stairs as there are, and along all those corridors, upper halls, and landings of the house. Decide whether natural daylight will help; if not, use concealed lights to create a welcome and an invitation to explore further.

One of the most welcoming halls I know uses concealed daylight from a source above the ground floor to flood light onto the staircase. It is nearly impossible not to be drawn to it. Similarly, objects lit up in corridors and bright lights beckoning from darker tunnels are ways to make visitors feel enthusiastic.

Indeed, properly treated, staircases and landings can be magical places at night, filled with angles, shadows, flickers, and mystery. The skill is to create an atmosphere both by day and night, taking advantage of spaces which, unlike the main rooms of a house, do not reveal themselves all at once. You can offer promises—but you must fulfill them.

THIS PAGE Huge windows are at their best on staircases, which is why they have been used since the 17th century in this way. This modern version—with its interesting pattern of glazing bars and an individual wooden door—occupies an entire wall. More light floods in from an adjoining room with another huge area of glass.

INSET If you have too much light, reduce it by using a large object in silhouette to draw attention to the view beyond.

THIS PAGE Though such blue-and-white Staffordshire pottery was never intended to be hung on a wall, blue and white makes a highly decorative scheme when used well. Note how the walls are just a shade softer than the blue of the pottery.

OPPOSITE, ABOVE LEFT The invention of the oil lamp in the 19th century led to some extraordinarily robust shapes and patterns. This collection has exuberant upturned shades in many varieties. The whole is used to add interest to a dull corner.

OPPOSITE, ABOVE RIGHT The owner of this house by the water loves to collect pictures of ferns and can't resist a tiny apprentice's chair when she finds one. Collections like this should be massed together for maximum impact.

OPPOSITE, BELOW RIGHT Mirrors are perfect for halls and corridors because they collect any available light and double it. They echo unseen views, which creates extra interest in narrow spaces. It is also practical to have a mirror as you leave or arrive at home. This owner has added a quirky bowl of apples, poised on a high stool.

DISPLAY

USE THOSE DIFFICULT AREAS UNDER THE STAIRS TO MAKE AN IMMEDIATE STATEMENT. THIS IS WHERE YOU CAN POSE A HUGE PIECE OF SCULPTURE, A GILDED PALAZZO SOFA TOO HARD TO SIT ON, A FAIRGROUND GALLOPER, OR A GIGANTIC AMMONITE.

What miserable places staircases and halls would be without pictures. Think of those soulless offices where the limit of imagination is to have the walls decorated with tiny contrasting paint spots, apparently blown on by a fly spray—or industrial warehouses where everything is made of concrete and then painted hard gloss green and cream. As you set off upstairs, you are followed by a dismal echo. These transient spaces where people never sit and contemplate are ideal for a shifting display. First, the walls cry out for interest. Second, the more you put on them, the gentler the

acoustic will be. Third, because no one ever lingers long on stairs, the display can be eccentric, challenging, and changing without giving offense.

My stairs and landings are stuffed with pictures—though it can take months, even years, to put them back after repainting. Unlike the walls of rooms, staircase walls are continuous and strange shapes. Pictures therefore need to climb their way up with conviction. And, if you want to change the mood—from 18th-century prints, say, to colorful modern abstracts—you will have to find a way of doing so. In this case, try to find 18th-century prints that look abstract and a monochrome abstract which, from a distance, might be 18th century. Not easy, but possible. For some reason, monochrome works well in these spaces, probably because, whatever the subject, the controlled palette is common to all.

If you can afford it (and frames may cost far more than the pictures), using frames in a single style is effective. Try sticking to plain black, which works with almost everything, or simple silver or gold. Common subject matter is another unifier—be it animal prints, engineering drawings, or portraits of children.

Mirrors make for excellent display in these areas as well as helping to turn corners. They will not only echo the groups on upper and lower walls (and give you the chance to check your outfit), but will increase light in dark areas if carefully positioned.

You can also hang other objects on your staircase and landing walls, but because space is usually confined here, they will have to be quite shallow—though they can be large. Indeed, the staircase often has the largest wall space in the house. Objects also need to be firmly attached to the walls because so much is carried up and down. Try wrestling with an Eames-style chair with rotating steel foot and you will soon see what damage can be done by flicking precious pieces off the wall.

You can also mix pictures with objects, especially if they have a connection. For example, try matching large oil paintings of stags with real antlers, or botanical drawings of lilies with identical, but living, plants on nearby furniture. Mix schoolbook prints of dinosaurs with collected fossils.

The objects do not, of course, need to be stuck on the walls. They can be positioned on small pieces of furniture, which will help dress up a forlorn landing, or ranged on narrow shelves put up for the purpose. It is possible to buy U-shaped shelves that are extremely narrow but whose outer lip stops photos and objects from sliding off.

OPPOSITE, LEFT Every nation appears to have its own straw hat, from coolie to Panama. Examples of these hats have been arranged to good decorative effect in this hall.

LEFT Paintings and photos of disparate shapes, sizes, and styles can be made uniform by clever framing. The style of frame needs to be nearly identical (but not quite), while the area of each mat should be roughly in equal proportion in each picture. This subtle group benefits from the odd-one-out set near the center.

RIGHT Convex mirrors popular in the Regency period were never intended to be used as looking glasses. They are purely decorative and give a fisheye view over huge areas of corridor. Use them to add emphasis and to catch both the eye and the light.

BELOW This monochrome scheme on a smallish staircase landing will cause people to pause and look at the photographs displayed at eye level. Each is given a simple frame—though no two are identical—and neutral mats.

THOSE TRANSIENT SPACES WHERE PEOPLE NEVER SIT AND CONTEMPLATE ARE IDEAL FOR A SHIFTING DISPLAY.

Stairs and halls are also useful if you have good-looking objects to display. Someone I know with a tiny apartment uses landings as closets—but she is abnormally neat. I use my stairs as a dumping ground for books and magazines going up to the living room or down to the office, but it is possible to keep long runs of glossy magazines piled on each stair tread, a year at a time. Runs of good-looking paperbacks are even better, because they are narrow enough not to impede the tread.

Clever storage gurus have invented elegant baskets of willow or colored sisal that fit into the stairs and can be filled with, for example, files or needlework. Indeed, many everyday objects look highly attractive if carefully chosen and grouped. Make a gallery of family photographs circling up the stairs, or imitate restaurants and have a giant bowl of wrapped candy on a hall table, looking elegant and welcoming.

Use your matching luggage as storage up the stairs, starting with briefcases and small suitcases and working up to an old trunk on a wide landing. Hats are obvious for display as are hats, riding boots and walking canes. You may find silver-topped ebony beauties in antique markets. I've also seen such mundane household items as brooms, aluminum trash cans, and laundry boxes displayed here with flair.

OPPOSITE **Displaying objects doesn't necessarily mean a huge group or pile of clutter. The wide, white walls of this spacious hall are hung with a single abstract sculpture of muted colors. The genius here is to position this sculptural chair directly beneath it.**

ABOVE LEFT **Displays don't have to be expensive or rare. A set of shallow shelves at the top of an attic staircase are decorated with a series of pebbles. Any beach or river will yield scores of well-washed, rounded stones. They may be chosen for sentimental reasons or simply for their beauty.**

ABOVE **An advantage of propping pictures on a shelf, as in this minimalist hall, is that they can be changed at whim. Such an idea would suit someone with a constantly changing set of prints or photos – or anyone with a wall made of such tough material that a picture nail cannot be driven into it.**

RIGHT Even in a small house or apartment, you can create extra storage in unexpected areas—and it can be made to look good, too. The designer who lives in this house believes that her rooms are better left uncluttered, so she has decided to use what would otherwise be wasted spaces on landings and stairways to store her working equipment. A collection of matching but cheap rush baskets holds anything from shoes to files, while magazines are piled in other purpose-built boxes. Better-looking shoes are laid out on display.

STORAGE

YOU CAN HIDE OR FLAUNT YOUR STORAGE—AND THERE IS PLENTY IN FAVOR OF EITHER SOLUTION. HIDDEN CUPBOARDS IN CORRIDORS AND LANDINGS WILL ENCOURAGE A FEELING OF SPACE. FLAUNTED SHELVES AND CUPBOARDS WILL, BY CONTRAST, REDUCE SPACIOUSNESS, BUT ADD A GREAT DEAL OF INTEREST.

Despite the supposed advent of the paperless office over a decade ago, we seem to be deluged with more bits of paper than ever before. Indeed, we seem to be deluged with more of everything. As a result, more storage is needed rather than less—and that is where hallways, corridors, and staircases can really come into their own. We often don't think about such spaces, and the result is that they go to waste. The cupboard under the stairs is filled with a couple of brooms, a vacuum cleaner, and some old dustcloths, all gathering cobwebs; the landings are, at best, an area for hanging pictures and objects—and, at worst, a gloomy no-man's-land where objects silt up waiting to find their resting place. Corridors are left entirely unregarded.

But in the last few years designers everywhere have been rethinking where we should keep everything from family archives to fax machines—with the result that there are many elegant solutions for storing difficult objects.

One of the most obvious solutions—ideal for under-the-stair spaces—are those matching sets of boxes and baskets that are widely available. I have vast quantities of elegantly covered boxes, some in differently patterned but similarly colored fabrics (it is a good idea to be able to tell from the outside what is inside), which can be piled on top of each other, with the most often used at the top. Charming old suitcases, piled on each

ABOVE Some shelves in this designer's home are adorned with carefully arranged painted shapes, while others are stacked with huge collections of magazines. Another part of the landing has been adapted for use as a closet. The lack of fuss and shades of white (even the stairs are white) transforms the practical into the beautiful.

RIGHT This entrance hall has been given rustic treatment. A basket of logs, a little spray of country-garden flowers, and a flouncy lampshade, together with the antique furniture, all set the scene. The fact that this is a working area is discreetly concealed.

THIS PAGE Some corridors and landings have been given generous amounts of space that can be put to use. Many are ideal storage areas: they benefit from the extra interest of cupboards and shelves while at the same time freeing living rooms from clutter. This built-in set of cupboards incorporates a radiator and allows for a display above head height. A basket is always useful as a halfway house for objects on their way up or down.

YOU CAN BORROW SPACE FROM A GENEROUS CORRIDOR OR LANDING AND LINE IT WITH CAPACIOUS BUILT-IN CABINETS.

other or sitting on the stairs, are another option. Even better would be a form of bookshelves specially designed for such boxes so that all of them can be easily accessed. Shelves would also organize the space with efficiency. In this case, I'd suggest that all the boxes should be exactly the same, giving the impression of a wall, with, on the shelves beneath, card holders describing their contents. It would be nicer still to have such personal record holders made to order—in marbled paper, perhaps, or one's own choice of fabric—but I have to confess I have yet to find any firm to make them at reasonable cost. But I do happen to know that many of the British royal family's archives, letters, and drawings are kept in fine, sturdy boxes covered in scarlet buckram and surmounted by the royal arms. They are made in-castle, so to speak, and work wonders.

While boxes look good in urban spaces, baskets are the choice for country homes. They also have the advantage of always being handmade. Most countries have resident basket makers who will create them to whatever size you want. I've had this done with chestnut shavings in Italy, where the baskets live on shelves made from plastered breeze blocks surfaced with terra-cotta tiles, and in fine English willow in Britain, where basket makers live near their trees.

The cheapest baskets of all come from the East where bamboo and rattan are woven in an extraordinary variety of shapes and sizes. It is worth looking at what's on offer ready-made and deciding whether it is cheaper to get the baskets to fit the shelves or the shelves to fit the baskets.

Spaces in corridors can also be used for storing books and magazines. Indeed, an entire wall of bookcases in halls or landings will unify the space, help insulate the area, and add interest to a dull wall. If you are building shelves especially, figure out exactly what height each should be for maximum coverage. The smallest shelves, for paperbacks, should be at the top, with the space increasing (and, if necessary, the depth, too) as they descend. If the corridor or level under the stairs gets really high, fill the tops with books more beautiful than readable, or a series of objects or pictures. Alternatively, have a library ladder or steps to make full use of the area.

Using these awkward spaces needs lateral thinking. Look at what you need to store and ask whether, for instance, it is really

ABOVE A built-in closet has been given an interesting pattern by a series of upright glazing bars set into their upper section—which still manage to conceal whatever chaos may be behind them. Note how the stripe of the carpet takes up the motif, and how the pretty chair is placed for maximum impact.

RIGHT Anyone who has lived in a multistory house will be well aware of the value of having storage on each landing. While being full of verve, this set of colorful suitcases can also be used to conceal books, laundry, or mail on its way to a different floor. Filled with clean sheets, they can even be carried up and down.

essential to have your clothes in the bedroom. Probably not, especially if, like me, you dress in the bathroom. Maybe you need some there, but out-of-season ones will fit in other gaps. Does kitchen equipment have to be in the kitchen? Maybe, but not those large fish steamers and rice cookers. They, too, could be usefully hidden in boxes in the hall.

Other annoying articles might also be neatly stowed away in under-stair spaces or little-used corridors. Think of bikes and buggies, garden tools, watering cans, and wheelbarrows, and take a leaf from the Shakers, who hung everything from pegs. Even bicycles can be hung up on wall pegs and look good if treated as sculpture. And it certainly stops you from falling over them at night.

If all else fails, you can simply borrow space from a generous corridor or landing and reduce its width by anything from 6 in to 3 ft (15 cm to 1 m) with built-in cupboards. These can be as obvious as you like. You can make them into features with paneling, cut glass handles, or sections of shelves covered with objects. You can design them to

seem like 18th-century painted cupboards or give them a top like a hutch and decorate it with pottery or glasses (another space saved in the kitchen).

You can make them into print rooms by sticking black and white prints to the doors, or copy scrap screens and stick on multicolored pictures cut from magazines or comics. Add botanic prints or team colors. Behind the closed doors, there may be children's toys or rows of shoes, essential but obsolete bunches of papers, or all those awkwardly-shaped objects that can't be thrown out.

Cabinets can incorporate radiators by having sections with ornamental grilles in wood or metal, and leave space at the top for large baskets or objects that are good-looking enough to stand inspection.

Finally, these cabinets can be almost hidden from view by making them plain, with flush doors, and blending them in with nearby walls. Build them so that they fit snugly from floor to ceiling and are the length of the corridor (leave space for doors to open at each end). You can take the trickery even further, by

OPPOSITE, LEFT The bicycle in the hall used to be a cliché for uncomfortable apartment-dwelling life—you always stumbled over the pedals of the next-door resident. Here, the cliché has been turned into decoration with bikes hung on wall racks. Somehow, even the abandoned balls look good.

OPPOSITE, RIGHT The storage cupboards in this early 20th-century house become almost invisible when painted in with the all-white walls. The stool and glass brick wall attract the eye, as do the two objects on the intervening shelf. The cold effect of pure white everywhere is avoided by adding a bowl of brilliant oranges.

LEFT If you are lucky enough to have a corridor too wide for your needs, build in a long closet. The series here starts just above baseboard level and stop short of the ceiling, but the full-height doors and lack of handles mean that they are nearly invisible.

BELOW Coats in a bedroom closet can be annoying. Not only do they demand a long drop, but often they need to be carried up and down stairs from the bedroom. The answer is to have a concealed closet as near the entrance door as can be arranged. This one would normally be concealed, with nothing but a small handle to give it away.

LEFT A large but quietly painted mirror distracts attention from what is a major storage area, judging by the capacious closet that can be seen reflected in it. The mirror stands on a box, which is also a useful place to secrete rarely wanted objects. Shoes and bag add to the casual but decorative feeling.

BELOW White-painted tongue-and-groove boards disguise good storage space under the stairs. The diamond-shaped abstract on the top cupboard diverts attention, as do the oil lamps casually dotted on the floor. Sensibly, the main cupboard is easily accessible.

RIGHT Although the books piled in this understairs area are both messy and clearly well used, they do not detract from the elegant sweep of the stairs above. The reason is that the striped chairs take first place, with the heavy struts of the shelves adding to the geometry. The books are almost an afterthought.

IF YOU GIVE HALLS, UNDERSTAIRS SPACES, AND LANDINGS TIME AND THOUGHT, THEY WILL REPAY THE EFFORT BY NOT ONLY LOOKING GOOD BUT ALSO WORKING WELL.

hanging pictures on them (screwed with brackets at each side so they don't fall off when the doors are opened), or if the doors are rarely used, putting small tables or chairs in front.

Flaunted storage may not be what it appears. Cupboards and hutches, for instance, may conceal freezers and washing machines in the closed areas below the shelves. Closed bureau bookcases and tallboy lookalikes in painted composite board may seem perfect pieces of hallway furniture but hide distressing secrets behind their deliberately distressed doors.

I once was hired to visit and write about all the suites in four of London's greatest hotels. The top designers commissioned to style these premium areas had created masterpieces of concealment, from gingham-covered Provençal chests which held massive TVs to Chinese lacquer cabinets secreting the cocktail tray. You can do the same, whether by building

cabinets onto the walls or using freestanding antiques. There are lots of Chinese lacquer chests on the market that are narrow enough for halls, along with small 18th-century chests of drawers that may still cost less than purpose-made shelves. Put the chest under a huge mirror for a stunning effect.

These spaces lend themselves to the grand style, whether ancient or modern, and it is surprising how many different ways they can be put to good use. The trick is to make sure bought furniture is the proper scale and depth to look right and suit your purpose, while custom-made shelving must be carefully planned to be of maximum value.

Halls and landings are nearly always unconsidered spaces because people simply ignore their potential. If you give them time and thought, they will repay the effort by not only looking good but also working well.

RIGHT Halls are complicated to furnish because they can be strangely proportioned: over-high, over-narrow, oversized. A good solution is to go for a piece of furniture that makes a statement on its own. This eccentric old armoire—strange enough to be a sculpture—is a perfect example.

FAR RIGHT This settee is another example of a fine piece of hall furniture. Influenced by 18th-century Swedish taste, it has a naively elegant silhouette that is perfect against a large wall, especially in this leaf green.

FURNISHINGS

WITHIN THE CONSTRAINTS OF SPACE—AND THIS MAY MEAN TOO MUCH SPACE AS WELL AS TOO LITTLE—IT IS ENORMOUS FUN TO FURNISH HALLS AND CORRIDORS (THOUGH STAIRCASES MAY BE INTRACTABLE). THIS IS BECAUSE THERE IS NO NEED TO BE SEVERELY PRACTICAL. FURNITURE HERE SHOULD BE TREATED AS DISPLAY AND GIVE A TASTE OF THE STYLE OF THE REST OF THE HOUSE.

It is tempting to leave the hallways and stairs of your house a clutter-free zone. But, believe me, you shouldn't. These areas provide a wonderful opportunity not only for showing off your design talents, but also for creating small niches to use for different purposes on different days.

My first house had a minuscule room created by stairs leading down to a cellar, and we furnished it with a small table, two Regency chairs, and a tiny bookcase. We sat there with a glass of wine on Saturday mornings because it was the only room in the house that looked out over the backyard—and we loved it.

There may be a small area in your home that is the only place where you can bask in the sun at noon on a cold midwinter's day—so you need to think carefully about the furnishings. It could be a large landing at a point where the stairs dog-leg up or a hall high in the eaves looking out over the rooftops. I have seen such areas decked with truly showy bureau bookcases and transformed into serious offices. Bureau bookcases are perfect in this kind of spot because, while grand in style, they are narrow.

OPPOSITE, BELOW The combination of elegant furniture and scoured floorboards in this good-sized hall is very much of today. The console table with its cabriole legs and ornate carving is grand enough to stand alone, but the mirror—which hangs from baseboard level rather than above the table—draws even more attention to its curves. The mirror also echoes the arch of the corridor beyond.

THIS PAGE A piece of furniture from any period can be made welcome in a hall as long as it has the character to be a bit of a showoff. This colorful cabinet dating from the mid-20th century is perfect for the job. It is forceful, subtly colored, and allows floor and baseboard to be seen beneath its main bulk. Note how the colors in the picture above echo the colors in the cabinet below.

ABOVE Peasant furniture was often designed to fit in narrow poky spaces, so it is useful in corridors and landings. Much of it is naive, homemade, and pleasingly chunky. This cabinet keeps its distressed soft green paint, emphasized by the vase on its top.

ABOVE RIGHT Furniture does not need to be freestanding; it can be built in. Here, an old doorway—complete with molded frames and ornamental paterae—has been converted into a small "window-seat" without the window, and decorated with panels typical of the 18th century.

OPPOSITE, BELOW LEFT A shallow but wide half-landing has been put to use by placing this country-made settee against the wall. Its entertaining and naive shape is seen to maximum effect against the white, and an iron candelabra completes the picture.

OPPOSITE, BELOW RIGHT The Chinese made lots of long narrow tables, which are ideal in long narrow corridors. I know—I have one myself. Called altar tables, they vary from extremely plain to highly carved. This version has just a small decorative touch to reveal its provenance.

When you are trying to furnish the nooks and crannies that stairs and landings offer, the first thing to consider is scale. My little stairway room was too small for anything but the tiniest piece—but that didn't mean it had to be boring. Our Regency chairs were designed for the bedroom, and they were light in character but full of style. Today, I would cover their drop-in seats with something imaginative like faux zebra.

Painted Scandinavian-style chairs (you can find them in secondhand stores and distress the paintwork) are small but distinctive, and can be teamed with the rest of the decor—another tip when dealing with confined spaces. Console tables are good for table lamps and a small row of books, as are the charming rattan pieces currently being imported. If you want more storage for books because this area has to operate as an office, wall-mounted shelves look less bulky than floor-standing bookcases. Again, try to blend them in with the paintwork.

Smallish areas do not always demand small pieces of furniture. On occasion, you can make a grand statement. The most obvious of these is a hallway mirror, which takes up no space but creates a big impact. If you have a high ceiling, find or make an enormous mirror that hangs from floor to ceiling. Position it so it maximizes the light and space of the area by apparently extending corridors and reflecting daylight back from windows opposite. If you have a bit more space, the mirror can be

THERE MAY BE A SMALL
AREA IN YOUR HOME
THAT IS THE ONLY PLACE
WHERE YOU CAN BASK IN
THE SUN AT NOON ON A
COLD MIDWINTER'S DAY.

RIGHT A Napoleon chair—based on a design by Sir Edwin Lutyens—fits perfectly into this corner of an upstairs hall. Upholstered in black horsehair, it was designed so people could sit comfortably with their legs dangling over one side. Beside the chair and underneath it are piles of books for browsing, creating a cozy library space.

169

propped against a wall, slanting up to catch the line of the stairs. In each instance, make sure that the mirror is safe—they can be very heavy and potentially dangerous. In larger halls, a mirror can be hung behind another piece of furniture—a table or console, which is then used to double the effect of lighting and display by reflection. Indeed, it is almost a cliché to have a mirror in the entrance hall—but it is a cliché worth putting up with since there is a purpose to it. Not only does this mirror maximize the light in what often tends to be a dark space, but you can also use it to check your appearance before you leave the house.

Entrance halls should also have somewhere to deposit coats, shopping, and umbrellas—not just for yourself, but also for visitors. A pair of chairs on either side of the mirror or table is a good solution, as is a longer row of matching chairs. If you are relying on secondhand finds, paint them to complement the rest of the decor. I have a gigantic Chinese altar table that is 12 ft (4 m) long but less than 1 ft (30 cm) deep. The only place it can go is in the entrance hall because it is too unwieldy to go up stairs (hence it was good value).

When you are furnishing the halls and landings of your home, make sure you reflect the spirit of the place—though how a Chinese altar table works in an English Georgian townhouse I don't know. Where the style is sophisticated and elegant, the furniture should be along similar lines, but it doesn't have to be come from same period. Where you are dealing with heavy stonework and medieval beams, large and chunky tables and chairs will look especially good—though, curiously, 20th-century Bauhaus works in these situations, too. And it is clever, when matching furniture with sensuously curving stairs, to find pieces that curve in their own right.

OPPOSITE, LEFT Although the 19th-century staircase, with its ornate iron banisters, and the 20th-century sofa beneath are at least a century apart in date, both have sensuously relaxed curves—which is why the group works so well together. It may be unlikely that anyone will ever sit here, but the table and forceful arrangement make a small room out of a difficult space.

LEFT Again, the combination of a strictly classical 18th-century London hall and an Art Deco-style console table—this one was made in the late 20th century—has a powerful impact that springs from the affinity of styles. Both elements are monochrome and characterized by luxury and restraint. Hall furniture is most effective when it has a good silhouette and a strong presence.

ABOVE With skill, the awkward niches that turn up in halls and landings can be turned to positive advantage. This built-in settee has the decorative feature of a carved wooden end, not unlike a banister, which is silhouetted against a high window. The cushions, natural, plain, and welcoming, have been carefully chosen to harmonize with the white wood.

BELOW The stump of a tree—which looks as though it grew on the balcony before the curved wall and integral slit window were even thought of—has been transformed into a characterful landing seat.

BOTTOM Often the choice and placing of furniture is instinctive. Did the owners of this hall notice how the vertical slats of the simple chair and the nearby wooden table mirrored the horizontal beams of the ceiling?

SMALL AREAS DON'T ALWAYS NEED SMALL PIECES OF FURNITURE. ON OCCASION YOU CAN MAKE A GRAND STATEMENT.

There are plenty of pieces of furniture that are seriously impractical but very beautiful, especially if well lit. I recently bought a Chinese medicine cabinet—22 small drawers, each covered with a worn Chinese ideogram. Since it is narrow and virtually useless—more a show-off than anything else—it is hall furniture par excellence. So are the fine black lacquered cabinets that have recently reappeared from China and wonderful Art Deco pieces of shagreen, tortoiseshell, and silver gilt.

Although such wonders may upset your financial advisor, you need only one distinctive piece to set the scene. If you prefer to keep the money manager happy, almost any secondhand find can be used here—good-looking sofas with broken springs, wobbly tables, impossible chairs.

Favor looks above comfort. If you are trying to create little oases up and down the stairs, one way to delineate them is to change the floor covering. Carpets are out of fashion now, so you will probably be inclined to leave these areas uncarpeted or part-covered by runners, both in the halls and up the stairs, even though it is less practical than the wall-to-wall option.

If the main area of the hall is, say, covered with a square of seagrass matting, then an area with a sofa under the stairs could be given its own oriental rug. If the stairs are left as polished or painted wood, the small sitting area by the main window could have a kilim both on a window seat and the floor. The change of flooring makes a niche seem like a proper room.

LEFT Only recently have curves been given full play in interiors, partly because new inventions allow them and partly because concrete came into its own in the 20th century. Here, instead of squared-off banisters at the top of a staircase, a series of curved half-walls undulate along a corridor. A Modernist chair has been tucked into a niche, its colors matching the rough logs beyond.

THIS PAGE Window seats are always welcome where there is a good view—whether of rolling fields or street life below. In this example, a wide area of a landing has been chopped off to create a generous cushioned area. The wood of window, walls, and banisters has been left a pleasant soft shade, and a welcoming lantern hangs from each side of the revere.

DOORS

WHATEVER ELSE HALLWAYS AND LANDINGS LACK, THEY ALL HAVE PLENTY OF DOORS. A MAJOR ROOM CAN EXIST WITH ONLY A SINGLE DOOR, BUT THE SERVICE PASSAGES OF A HOUSE MAY CONTAIN UP TO A DOZEN DOORS OPENING ONTO VIRTUALLY EVERY SINGLE ROOM.

If halls and other important but undervalued spaces are to be treated properly, all the doors in each space should be given the same design elements. In some houses—either those that have had servants' or old-fashioned nursery areas, or those that combine features from a mixture of periods—the style of door may vary considerably.

In our Jacobean house in Yorkshire, the front door was made of 17th-century oak planks, never painted, while the back door was paneled in late Georgian times with even later glass. Doors in the corridors were generally six-paneled affairs in the Georgian style, though some were of distinctly higher quality than others. Then, for warmth, we added a door in the corridor that was basically a single hefty glass plate.

How is one to treat such a miscellany? The answer is that all the doors within a certain section of the house should match as coherently as possible while keeping their own style. In this case, the old oak door remained untouched as a fine period piece, but all the other doors that led off a series of continuous corridors were treated with variations on the same theme. The inside back door, the glass door, and a single door into a different part of the house were painted plain white because all of them were connected with a white corridor. Once the inner corridor color changed to lemon yellow, the door panels and their surrounds were altered to two shades of gray while retaining their white frames. This

ABOVE LEFT Where the outside meets the interior is the place for a formal bit of topiary to welcome guests. Though the door is not glazed, a window alongside gives the impression it is.

ABOVE CENTER The strong upright glazing bars of this door frame the view. The eye is drawn to them and then the countryside beyond.

ABOVE RIGHT Double doors are wonderfully accommodating: in summer, one door can be left open to integrate the outdoors into the whole scheme; in winter, the doors can be firmly closed against the elements.

LEFT If you are too disciplined to allow circulars to drop to the floor in a messy way, the answer is to attach a bicycle or fishing basket just below the mail slot. It also changes an ugly area into something quirky and amusing.

OPPOSITE By choosing objects that are beautiful in themselves, workaday areas around front and back doors can be made into stylish features. This back door is obviously used as a log store and way into the yard—note the straw hats and the French basket for summer weeding—but even the brooms and logs contribute to a charming picture.

FAR LEFT, ABOVE AND BELOW
Doors need hardware—handles, locks, knockers, hinges—and decorative pieces in period can be particularly attractive. In a wood-frame house, where timber is paramount, both handles and locks can be made of wood in the medieval manner. Wooden dowels (below), once regularly used instead of nails and screws, look both authentic and decorative.

LEFT, ABOVE AND BELOW The modern passion for simplicity has brought popularity to the hidden closet or space where obtrusive and ugly objects can be concealed. Nothing works better in this situation than sliding doors, taken from floor to ceiling, with high-quality runners to make opening and closing easy. Here (below), the runners have been made into a pleasant decorative detail.

RIGHT Muted but complementary colors of soft grayish blue and citrus yellow make an area filled with built-in closets come alive. The conformation of doors and storage is both simple and complex.

was variation enough to give some sense of movement in the house without banging people over the head with violent change and disruption.

This kind of scheme works equally in a multistoryed townhouse where the doors may become less detailed as they venture into former servants' areas (no political correctness about equality in the 18th century). Whereas the main doors of the house can be colored to emphasize the architectural detailing, the less grand ones should be left a simple—but matching—color.

On the whole, I am not in favor of leaving modern wood doors unpainted. New wood can be a horrid strong tan color which no one would seriously choose. The effect can be lightened with white wash or a stain in some soft shade, or the whole can be painted. Gloss paint, by the way, is currently very unfashionable.

Old wood is quite a different matter. With age, most hard woods, from oak to mahogany, fade and bleach. Oak goes a splendid dark gray; teak a soft, pale gray; and mahogany, left in the sun, becomes dark beige. It also loses its characteristic gleam, which always gives away reproduction mahogany doors. All these ancient doors should be left exactly as they are. You cannot beat genuine aging.

HARD WOODS FADE AND BLEACH WITH AGE. OAK TURNS A SPLENDID DARK GRAY, TEAK GOES A SOFT PALE GRAY, AND MAHOGANY, LEFT IN THE SUN, BECOMES DARK BEIGE AND LOSES ITS GLEAM.

Softwood doors will almost certainly have been painted in their lives—probably so often that much of the sharpness of the carpentry has vanished. My inclination would be gradually to strip off these layers until you come, with luck, to the original paint color. If you can save bits of it in cracks and and panels, it will also give a fine effect of age. A good soft waxing will also bring out the grain of the wood underneath and add a glow.

The degree of distressing of a newly painted door depends on how rural an effect you desire. If the house doors are highly detailed, peeling paint is probably unsuitable (not always—consider a Dublin townhouse that is all peeling paint and wonderful with it). But, in the case of farmhouses, cottages, boathouses, and barns, a certain amount of applied wear looks good.

Local habits in coloring doors, especially outside, are also worth taking into account. An extreme example is a city square where all the door exteriors are the same color (I live in a square where all the doors are black). An exterior treatment may dictate how you treat the door inside, too. It is also important to try to fit in with custom and practice if you are buying a second home. In Italy, for instance, the cult of spanking new gloss paint does not, happily, exist. Most houses have interior and exterior doors where the paint gradually fades into a mellow shadow of its aggressive new self.

Everything is governed by fashion—even if one reacts violently against the current fad—and at present we are painting corridor and hall doors a darker shade than the walls. This has been inspired by the late 1990s craze for Shaker design and all things Colonial–styles that both had their roots in northern Europe. The soft blue colors of many doors and hallway furniture comes from Gustavian Sweden, while darker shades of brown and red are typical of northern Germany.

Coloring doors and woodwork a darker shade allows you both to make the walls even lighter without glare and to introduce a strong color to an undistinguished area. Plain white walls with plain flat-white doors may be fine in a minimalist warehouse, but they are definitely not cozy.

RIGHT The door is the making of this industrial-style stairway. While the metal stairs have been adapted hardly at all from functional factory ware, the huge door has clearly been designed with this particular space in mind. The small panes and heavy wooden glazing bars stop the eye and distract it from what is behind, while light can still flood onto the stairs.

FAR RIGHT, ABOVE Sliding doors have to be minimal or modern. This version, clearly inspired by Arts and Crafts style, has three virtues: light is borrowed from a sunny room beyond the hall; the large opening is good for furniture moving; and the doors look unexceptional when closed.

FAR RIGHT, BELOW This rather dull hallway has been transformed by the use of characterful doors: the black-and-white entrance door has a glass area beyond, allowing light but not drafts indoors, while the sliding French door makes a major statement in a small area.

WINDOWS

**IN MANY CASES OF STAIRWAY AND LANDING WINDOWS, A BLIND IS A GOOD OPTION, EVEN
THOUGH IT WILL BE LESS EFFECTIVE THAN CURTAINS IN REDUCING COLD AND NOISE. THE
ADVANTAGE OF A BLIND IS THAT IT TAKES UP LESS SPACE AND LIGHT AND GIVES COMPLETE
PRIVACY WHEN PULLED DOWN. IF THE VIEW FROM THE WINDOWS IS UNAPPEALING, A PLAIN
WHITE SHADE CAN BE LEFT CONSTANTLY PULLED AND LIGHT WILL STILL SHINE THROUGH IT.**

It is rare that stairway and landing windows are like those in other rooms. In some cases there is a single enormous window that stretches over more than one floor, filling the whole area with light and offering the best views over the yard. Many townhouses have similar arrangements—I've seen such windows in Bath, Edinburgh, and even the little Yorkshire fishing port of Whitby, where the long window was, unusually but wittily, shaped like a wine bottle. Don't ask why—this was an old bank.

Other buildings have different arrangements: stone castles and Lutyens-type vernacular stone houses may have a series of tiny windows climbing the walls as the stairs below them ascend; other houses, especially 20th-century modern, go for a series of asymmetrical rectangles, both shallow and deep.

None of these examples is easy to curtain, and perhaps the first way to treat your windows is just to let them be. If you are not especially overlooked and the heating works well, there is really no need to shut the panes off at night. Anyway, it is worth trying for a start, while you think about other—more expensive—ideas.

If, in the spell without curtains, you find the stairs and landings to be drafty, noisy or unfriendly, then it is best to go for the full curtain treatment—lined, interlined, weighted at floor level. This will not only keep out drafts, it will also soften the acoustics and look cozy and friendly. The style works best with impressively large

RIGHT This landing window looks stylish because the gingham curtains that have been chosen for the window are overscaled. The generously sized check gives the small landing a feeling of importance.

BELOW The whole point of this corridor is the heavy oak beams —which are clearly part of a timber-framed house. Sensibly, they have been emphasized at the expense of the rest of the corridor. The curtains at the end are in keeping but unobtrusive.

LEFT When you have a corridor as elegant and well lit as this one, you can afford to be extravagant with your design ideas. The theatrical curtains both emphasize the ranked windows and soften their effect. The curtains, drawn, will change a light-filled space into something dramatic but friendly.

BELOW AND BOTTOM The devil is in the detail. Nineteenth-century French metal valances are decoratively stamped and can be cut and nailed together to fit the space available. A heavy tassel makes a most decorative tieback, and these can be ordered in all sorts of different patterns.

windows, which are those that create the draft problem anyway. When you pick a fabric, go for plains, solids such as stripes and checks, or seriously overscaled patterns (a very expensive option, since the repeat will be huge). Avoid little cutesy designs. It is also a nice idea to splurge on the lining, which will be visible by day and at night from the outside.

Smaller-sized windows may look better if a single curtain is used to cover the whole area. One curtain will look less puny than two and will shut out less daylight when open. You can still make a curtain heavy and weighty and give it an attractive tieback—but don't extend it to the floor without careful thought.

The treatment of windows in halls and on large landings calls for something different. These are areas that may be used for a tiny office or a friendly meeting place, for an overstocked library, or other working area. These windows should be designed so the area looks like a real room—friendly, welcoming, and stylish. Take your cue from the rest of the house. If you are heavily into chintz or toile in the living room and bedroom, reflect this in the hall. If the house is thoroughly modern, go for sheers and plain fabrics.

In many cases of windows on stairways and landings, a blind or shade is a good option, but it will be less effective than curtains in reducing cold and noise. You can also opt for both shades and drapes, especially if you want privacy. The shade can be kept permanently closed (or drawn at night), while a heavy single curtain can be draped for effect in front. This need never be closed—which at least means that you can economize on the cost of the fabric.

WHEN PICKING A FABRIC FOR LARGE WINDOWS, GO FOR SOLIDS, PATTERNS THAT ARE WILDLY OVERSCALED, OR GEOMETRICS SUCH AS STRIPES AND CHECKS.

THIS PAGE **This extremely simple staircase manages to be both grand and friendly at the same time. The fine lines of the banisters and its rail are contrasted with the heavy, strong full-length curtains, and there is nothing but a decorative Indian hanging lamp for embellishment.**

RESOURCES

GENERAL

ABC Carpet & Home
881–888 Broadway
New York, NY 10003
For nearest store, call 561 279 7777
www.abchome.com
Exotic collection of home furnishings,
fabrics, carpets, and accessories.

Bloomingdales
1000 Third Avenue
New York, NY 10022
212 705 2000
www.bloomingdales.com
Department store; 24 locations
nationwide.

The Conran Shop
407 East 59th Street
New York, NY 10022
212 755 9079
www.conran.com
Cutting-edge design from furniture
to flatware.

Crate & Barrel
646 N Michigan Avenue
Chicago, IL 60611
800 996 9960
For nearest retailer, call 800 927 9202
www.crateandbarrel.com
Good-value furniture and accessories
from white china and glass to chairs.

IKEA
Potomac Mills Mall
2700 Potomac Circle, Suite 888
Woodbridge, VA 22192
For nearest store, call 800 254-IKEA
www.ikea.com
Home basics at great prices,
including assembly-kit furniture.

Macy's
800 BUY-MACY
www.macys.com
Department store; locations nationwide.
Furniture, accessories, etc.

Martha By Mail
P.O. Box 60060
Tampa, FL 33660-0060
800 950 7130
www.marthabymail.com
Tasteful homewares.

Neiman Marcus
For nearest store, call 888 888 4757
For mail order, call 800 825 8000
www.neimanmarcus.com
Department store; 31 locations
nationwide. Catalog.

Pottery Barn
P.O. Box 7044
San Francisco, CA 94120-7044
For nearest store, call 800 922 9934
www.potterybarn.com
Everything from furniture to decoration
details, such as china and pillows.

Restoration Hardware
935 Broadway
New York, NY 10011
212 260 9479
www.restorationhardware.com
Not just hardware; funky furnishings,
lighting, accessories.

Target Stores
33 South Sixth Street
Minneapolis, MN 55402
888 304 4000
www.target.com
Chain store with things both funky
and functional for the home.

Waverly
For dealer locations, call 800 423 5881
www.waverly.com
Decorative accessories including fabric,
wallpaper, and window treatments.

FABRIC FURNISHINGS

Anichini
466 North Robertson Boulevard
Los Angeles, CA 90048
800 553 5309
www.anichini.com
Fabrics, decorative pillows, and
upholstered sofas and chairs.

Calico Corners
203 Gale Lane
Kennett Square, PA 19348
800 213 6366
www.calicocorners.com
Retailer of fabric by designers such
as Waverly and Ralph Lauren, plus
furniture. Stores nationwide. Mail
order. Catalog.

DJC Design Studio
800 554 7890
www.djcDESIGN.com
Decorative pillows and throws.

The Fabric Center
485 Electric Avenue
Fitchburg, MA 01420
978 343 4402
A wide variety of decorator fabrics at
discounted prices. Mail order. Catalog.

Hancock Fabrics
2605A West Main Street
Tupelo, MS 38801
662 844 7368
www.hancockfabrics.com
America's largest fabric store.

Laura Ashley
For a retailer near you,
call 800 367 2000 or
visit www.lauraashley.com
Floral, striped, checked, or solid cottons.

On Board Fabrics
Route 27, P.O. Box 14
Edgecomb, ME 04556
207 882 7536
www.onboardfabrics.com
Everything from Balinese cottons to
Italian tapestry and botanical prints.

Oppenheim's
P.O. Box 29, 120 East Main Street
North Manchester, IN 469-62-0052
800 461 6728
Country prints, denim, chambray, flannel
fabrics, and mill remnants.

Silk Trading Co.
360 South La Brea Avenue
Los Angeles, CA 90036
800 854 0396, or visit
www.silktrading.com
More than 2,000 silk fabrics. Nine
stores nationwide. Catalog.

Tinsel Trading Co.
47 West 38th Street
New York, NY 10018
212 730 1030
Vintage to contemporary trims.

Thai Silks!
252 State Street
Los Altos, CA 94022
800 722 7455
www.thaisilks.com
Silk, velvet, organza, jacquard, and
taffeta. Mail order. Catalog.

PAINTS

Benjamin Moore & Co.
51 Chestnut Ridge Road
Montvale, NJ 07645
For distributors, call 800 826 2623
Many palettes, including 176 historic
paint selections.

Finnuren & Haley
901 Washington Street
Conshohocken, PA 19428
800 843 9800
The American Collection of historic
colors from the mid-1800s.

K-Mart
For nearest store, call 800 635 6278
www.kmart.com
256 everyday latex paint colors at
moderate prices, coordinated with
Martha Stewart home furnishings
available at K-Mart.

**McCloskey Special Effects
Decorative Finish Center**
6995 Bird Road
Miami, FL 33155
For distributors or nearest store,
call 866 666 1935/305 666 3300
www.o-geepaint.com/Faux/McFaux
Huge range of paints, finishes, glazes,
faux painting supplies.

Old Fashioned Milk Paint Co.
P.O. Box 222, Groton, MA 01450
For distributors or mail order,
call 978 448 6336
www.milkpaint.com
Manufacturer of authentic milk-paint
powders–add water and mix.

Shaker Workshops
P.O. Box 8001
Ashburnham, MA 01430-8001
For mail-order catalog,
call 800 840 9121/978 827 9000
www.shakerworkshops.com
Manufacturers of Shaker furniture;
Stulb's Old Village Paints sold in colors
to coordinate with Shaker tradition.

Sherwin-Williams Co.
101 Prospect Avenue, NW
Cleveland, OH 44115-1075
For distributors or nearest store,
call 800 474 3794
www.sherwin-williams.com
Manufacturers of Dutch Boy paints
and many special lines for specific
stores, such as K-Mart.